PRACTICING

COMPASSION

FRANK ROGERS JR.

FRESH AIR BOOKS

For Alane,

whose heart cascades,

like a Yosemite brook,

with love and compassion in abundance.

Upper Room Books® website: books.upperroom.org

FRESH AIR BOOKS® and design logos are trademarks owned by The Upper Room®, Nashville, Tennessee. All rights reserved.

Scripture quotations not otherwise noted are from the New Revised Standard Version Bible, copyright 1989 National Council of the Churches of Christ in the United states of America. Used by permission. All rights reserved.

At the time of publication all websites referenced in this book were valid. However, due to the fluid nature of the internet some addresses may have changed or the content may no longer be relevant.

Cover and interior design: Faceout Studio / faceoutstudio.com

ISBN 978-1-935205-25-8 (print)
ISBN 978-1-935205-26-5 (mobi)
ISBN 978-1-935205-27-2 (epub)

CONTENTS

EXERCISES

Acknowledgments

The Compassion Practice was birthed in a white-walled apartment by the San Francisco Bay in Sausalito. My gratitude is as boundless as the night sky we gazed upon from the porch our last night there. Andy Dreitcer, Mark Yaconelli, and Doug Frank, with Nancy Linton's wise spirit ever in our midst—you were the midwives who recognized that a baby was on the way and coaxed it into the world. There is no Compassion Practice without you.

The teachings and practices were developed and refined through the Triptykos School of Compassion at the Center for Engaged Compassion. Andy and Mark, teaching with you throughout the world will always be among the vocational highlights of my life. Doug and Nancy, the retreats we led are circles of grace that surfaced and seasoned the core of this work. The rest of the staff—Karri Backer, Rachel Fox, Jenn Hooten, Steve and Krystalynn Martin, and Cate Wilson—thank you for your interminable labor alongside your unshakable belief in this work. And Don Morrison of the Morrison Foundation—The Triptykos School itself was launched through your generous support. Thank you for your faith and your gift.

The Center for Engaged Compassion is housed at the Claremont School of Theology. I am grateful to President Jerry Campbell, Dean Philip Clayton, President Jeffrey Kah-Jin Kuan, Dean Sheryl Kujawa-Holbrook, and all the administrative staff who have unequivocally supported the center's work from the beginning. I am also grateful to the hundreds of students, retreatants, contemplative practitioners, social activists, and spiritual seekers who have given themselves to this work in seminary classes, weeklong retreats, pilot programs, healing and reconciliation workshops, and various compassion formation offerings through Triptykos and Claremont School of Theology. Your commitment to personal healing and social transformation not only inspire me; they give me hope.

Loved ones, friends, and colleagues read drafts of the manuscript: Mark, Andy, Doug, Nancy, Ulrike Guthrie, Jim Neafsey, Daniel Judah Sklar, Wendy Farley, Tom Rogers, Justin Rogers, and Alane Daugherty—thank you for your invaluable insight and encouragement. And from the beginning, the Upper Room staff have been understanding of the radical material, enthusiastic in their support, skillful in crafting a book to celebrate, and delightfully collegial through a process both pleasurable and energizing: Jeannie Crawford-Lee, John Mogabgab, Joanna Bradley, and Stephanie McGuirk—this book could not have found a better home.

Finally, I am graced beyond deserving for the family that sustains me. Alane, Justin, Michael, and Sammy, you teach me every day what true love and compassion looks like. And, Alane, you are the heart that holds it all. There is no me without you. As with everything else I have and am, this book is yours.

The Invitation

THE WAY OF
RADICAL COMPASSION

Compassion is the heartbeat of humanity.

We are most fully human, most fully ourselves, when we see someone in the truth of his or her experience and are moved to respond with kindness and care.

We glimpse a colleague smiling at his beloved's photograph, and our smile in response offers respite for us both from the whirlwind of the workday. We see our teenage daughter asleep on the couch, the cat curled up in her lap, and the wash of affection that comes over us reminds us of the love that ties us together. We see the same teenager, now late for school, frowning at her reflection in the mirror, and the morning's mad dash dissolves into the yearning that our child know the beauty we behold.

Pausing from the busyness of our lives and recognizing the tender humanity of another restores us to our own humanity. The pulse of care and connection within us resuscitates. Our hearts, normally dulled by the day's burdens, beat freely with love. And the ensuing kindness we extend to others has the power to resuscitate their spirits as well. For compassion not only restores the heart of our own humanity; its healing care makes human once more the heart of another grown hard and cold.

A Garden of Compassion

James Worthington knows such compassion.

James runs an inner-city youth program that offers young people an alternative to the deceptive lures of gang life. He tells his kids about Raul Torres, a former custodian in their own community. Raul lived with his wife of forty-five years on a modest corner lot in South Central Los Angeles. When his wife died of a stroke in her sleep, Raul was griefstricken. He retired from his job, sought solace from his church, and spent long hours staring at the yard from the porch his wife adored.

Raul decided to plant a memorial garden for his wife. It spanned the entire corner lot and contained flower beds ever in bloom, boxes of herbs and vegetables, tomatoes on the vine, cilantro in bundles, and rows of his beloved's favorite—prize-worthy roses of a dozen different hues. For Raul, the garden served as both a tender tribute and a second life in his later years.

One morning, Raul discovered that several rosebushes had been demolished. Shreds of blossom and bush were strewn on the ground as if they had been assaulted with a baseball bat. He was certain who had done it—a carload of local gang members had taken to cruising the place, driving by slowly and casing it with their cold, vacant stares.

Afraid of doing anything else, Raul simply swept up the mess, repaired the bushes, and tended the garden as if nothing had happened. Two days later, another bush was attacked. A few days later, yet another one. Angry and afraid, heartsick and powerless, Raul was beside himself about what to do. On the off chance it would deter the vandals, he sat in stoic vigil at the living room window.

That is when Raul saw the boy. He vaguely knew his story. The ten-year-old lived alone with his mother. His father had been gone for years and his brother, a gang member, was in jail for killing a rival. In retaliation for the murder his brother committed, a drive-by occurred at the boy's home. His leg was nicked by a bullet. Though scarcely limping any longer, the boy still walked with a cane. Raul watched him, presumably on his way to school. When he got to the roses, the boy wielded the cane like a weapon and lashed out at one of the bushes. Once done with the attack, he started to leave but then stopped. He noticed Raul staring from the window. The boy looked scared, as if caught with nowhere to go. Then he glared in defiance and swiftly scrambled away.

Raul's first instinct was to chase the boy down and scold him. His second was to call the police and turn the truant in. But he could not shake those eyes. It was as if Raul could see it all—the boy's aloneness, the rage, the terror, the futility, and lacing throughout, the despair that would make a future in gang life all but inevitable. Raul did not have the heart to turn the boy in. He let the boy's eyes haunt him until he had an idea.

That afternoon, Raul found the boy walking home from school and approached him. The boy hardened in defiance. Raul told him that he was having trouble with his garden—someone was destroying his flowers. The boy insisted it wasn't him, that he didn't know a thing about it. That wasn't what he meant, Raul assured him. He needed someone to help him protect the flowers and to help him care for them from time to time. He'd pay him, let him plant his own bushes, and teach him how to grow plants if the boy wanted. The boy was skeptical. Raul offered that they try it for one week. The boy just had to keep an eye on the garden, and on Saturday morning he would get paid.

On Saturday, the boy showed up. He stayed the better part of the day. Raul taught him how to tend roses and helped him plant a rosebush of his own. They harvested tomatoes and cut fresh herbs. At day's end, they picked a bag full of lemons and made fresh lemonade. It was the best the boy had ever tasted. It was so good, the boy came back the following week and the next.

To this day, James asserts, the garden has never been vandalized again. He would know—he's the boy who bludgeoned the roses. And this neighborhood is still his turf. It is where he works with other young people, offering them a place to flourish in the midst of the ever-present violence.

The Radical Invitation

When discussing compassion, we must be aware of the painful reality of our planet. We live in a violent world. Each day, lives and communities are ripped further apart by terrorist bombings and retaliatory attacks, school shootings and playground bullying, domestic abuse, gangland killings, even molestations in our sacred institutions. This violence bleeds into our relationships. Between loved ones at home, colleagues at the workplace, and adversaries dissenting in our political spaces, rage, resentment, blame, dismissiveness, and cycles of attack and withdrawal erode the very bonds on which love and community depend. And the violence cuts deeper still. It slices us open from the inside. Spite, disgust, anger, despair, fear, shame, loathing of others and ourselves consume us with such ferocity that we either act out, possessed by their power, or resist their grip through self-medication. We are a world at war, and the war is waged both within and without.

And yet.

In the midst of the world's brutality, a retired custodian named Raul shines as a beacon of compassion. His example shows us that in the midst of the violence around and within us, it is possible to recover and retain our humanity. However mundane or severe the conflicts or afflictions that burden us—feuds at the office, hostilities at home, offenses at the hands of a stranger—a path toward life and reconnection lies before us. The path is radical, but so is its promise. It uncovers genuine compassion—a compassion so healing it resuscitates the heart of a man stricken by grief and softens the heart of a boy hardened into despairing rage. This book describes that path. The path's invitation is threefold.

First, this path invites us to know, in the depths of our souls, a compassion that holds and heals us.

Even in the face of violence, sources of compassion continue to sustain our world. In spite of all the aloneness, alienation, cruelty, and coldness that pervade our broken planet, wellsprings of kindness and goodwill, like underground pools in a desert, offer healing, renewal, and sustenance. Compassion is birthed out of these springs. To give love, we have to know love. To be moved by the suffering or joy of another, our own suffering must be seen and our joy the object of someone's delight. In the absence of love, the heart hardens; in the presence of love, even the hardest of hearts can grow soft like clay massaged in a potter's hands.

We find such wellsprings of compassion all around—in a loved one's touch and a mentor's unfailing encouragement, in the kindness of strangers and the warmth of religious communities, in 12-step programs, contemplative retreats, a child's smile, a friend's embrace. Raul Torres found them in a spouse's care, in the gifts of the earth, in an evening's quiet, and weekly worship. A ten-year-old vandal found them in the face of a forgiving victim. For some, these springs are icons of a vast and cosmic presence of compassion that holds all of creation with infinite love. Cosmic or merely mortal, these pools of compassion are so empathic they hold with healing care our deepest wounds, our most secret shames. And they are so expansive that they hold and heal the bloodstained suffering even of one who would kill. The path of compassion reconnects us to the sources of life and love that sustain us. It invites us to see our reflection in the surface of these grace-filled pools and soak in the soothing waters until every tissue of our being knows we are held and healed in love.

Second, the path of compassion invites us to be liberated from the internal turbulence that disconnects us from our compassionate core.

Through most of our waking hours, emotions assail us—fear, anger, anxiety, and stress. Impulses drive us—to work, run errands, do chores, numb out. Internal monologues hound us—self-critique, perfectionism, blame, or judgment. All of these alienate us from the loving people we know ourselves to be. We seldom feel like we are at the tiller of our lives; rather, we feel hurled about by the winds of the moment, swallowing water within the swirling waves of the passions and voices that toss us from within.

As Raul Torres shows us, even within the riptides of such strong emotions as grief, despair, fear, and indignation, we can find a space of freedom from the tumult of our inner world. We can cultivate a grounded internal stability that quiets the cacophony, anchors our power, and restores our capacity for purposeful action. The power that stills these storms within is compassion, compassion turned inward. Self-compassion is the secret to interior freedom and personal restoration. The raging heart of a ten-year-old delinquent relaxes before a caring and understanding face. So too does the raging heart within us. When we extend to ourselves the understanding and care we would to a suffering child, the tempest within subsides, solid ground appears, and the way forward reveals itself to us. Self-compassion brings us home to ourselves.

Unfortunately, self-compassion is a rather rare commodity in our world. We do not love ourselves very well. Self-loathing, self-disgust, and self-castigation are obscenely epidemic. Think of the internal voices with which we berate ourselves: *You stupid idiot. How could you do such a shameful thing? If people ever saw what you are really like they would turn away in disgust.* If we ever attacked another with these words, it would rightly be considered abusive. The invitation that comes from Jewish and Christian spiritual paths, for example, is to love our neighbor *as* ourselves, not *instead of* ourselves. The care, goodwill, and delight we extend to ourselves should be the measure of that which we offer to others. Tragically, for most of us, this is a rather low bar.

The path of compassion offers an antidote to the self-hatred that consumes us. It invites us into a relationship with ourselves that truly knows ourselves as beloved; that holds our own shadows, shames, and internal furies with empathic understanding and healing love; and that restores us to the core of care that is the essence of who we are. Out of the abundance of such self-compassion we are able to have genuine compassion for others—indeed, to love our neighbors with the very same love with which we love ourselves.[1]

Third, the path of compassion invites us to feel genuine care toward others.

This is a care that sees others free from the distortions of our own fears and wounds. It recognizes the inherent dignity and unique beauty within all persons, even those most damaged; it is moved by others' suffering, however well hidden; and it extends a word or gesture of kindness that might ease their pain or foster the restoration of their beaten down humanity. Such connection and care can be cultivated toward colleagues in the workplace, loved ones at home, and the person next door or at the supermarket. In such moments, our hearts flow freely with the pulse of compassion. We feel human. We feel like ourselves.

The reach of compassion, however, extends radically further. As Raul Torres exemplifies, compassion can be cultivated not only toward our friends, allies, and associates but also toward our opponents, our enemies, people who trigger us, and people who accost us. In our fight-or-flight world, we are often convinced that our only two options in the face of aggression are retaliation or passivity. Whether in reaction to a loved one who yells at us, a coworker mistreating us, an adversary demeaning us, or an assailant violating the work of our hands, our response to assault defaults into counterattack or submissive endurance.

The path of compassion points to another way. To be sure, it is a way that stands up to violation—protects the vulnerable, empowers the victimized, holds offenders accountable, and restrains the unrepentant. However, it does so in ways that refuse to demonize the other, even those whose deeds are monstrous; that recognize the suffering of the attacker, though hidden underneath his or her attempts to inflict pain; and that invite the offender's restoration to the community on the condition he or she makes amends, even if only symbolically, and acts humanely. We can meet adversaries with empowered constraint, empathic understanding, and a genuine sense of restorative care. When we do, we retain our own humanity even when others remain marred by the inhumane.

Compassion is the means to becoming most deeply human. It revives the pulse of one depleted by heartbreak and suffering. It sustains the pulse of interior freedom and grounded empowered care. And it resuscitates the pulse of the person deadened by brutality, uniting him or her once more with the human community. Compassion is the heartbeat that restores life. Compassion is the bond of genuine connection.

Truth be told, however, compassion is difficult.

The Problem Is *How*

Kathy's inner world is so out of control it is making her physically sick. A highly successful businesswoman at a Fortune 500 affiliate, she lives in constant fear of being exposed for the incompetent imposter she believes she is. Anxiety all but paralyzes her when preparing a presentation. The slightest critique from her supervisor devastates her for days. Her own inner voice of self-contempt so savagely picks her apart, her only means to sleep at night is to munch on Tums and work until she drops. She knows she is acting irrationally. She graduated from Stanford *summa cum laude* and followed that with an MBA from Harvard. But it doesn't matter. She is driven to perfection, and she is painfully aware of how far she falls short.

Bill is a single dad with two teenaged boys. He loves them dearly. Bill holds down two jobs—a traveling sales rep by day, a web designer from the house by night. He comes home each evening with but a tiny window of time to connect with the boys, make dinner, check on homework, and attend to the most pressing of the household chores. All he asks is that they clean up their own messes before he gets home. They never do. The second he walks through the door, the sight of food wrappers and dirty dishes strewn from the kitchen counters to the family room coffee table infuriates him. He nags. They ignore him. He turns off the TV and yells. They sigh in disgust, toss dishes into the sink, and retreat to their bedrooms both shamed and defiant. Bill feels horrible—he is certain he is losing them—but he is defiant as well. His sons really do have to learn. Yet the only thing anyone learns is how to endure dinner in silence.

Maria's stepfather sexually abused her throughout her childhood. After years of therapy, she has created a stable life. More than a survivor, she is thriving—she is married, studying women's health, and raising a daughter of her own. For nearly ten years, however, she has refused to be in the same city with the man who violated her. Her religious friends have been little help, admonishing her to forgive and let go, telling her that her resentment will eat her from the inside out. Yet even the thought of him enrages her; the very word *forgiveness* makes her want to scream. Now, her younger brother is getting married and wants her daughter to be the flower girl. Both he and their mother implore Maria to bring her family to the wedding. She is genuinely torn. She loves her brother, and her daughter would be thrilled. But that man sitting next to her mother ignites a fury inside her that wants to torch the entire event. How does she care for both herself and her family when her abuser remains present and unrepentant?

How indeed.

The call for compassion arises from all quarters of our society. Peace-keeping agencies appeal for compassion in resolving escalating hostilities internationally. Civic leaders plead for more compassion within the demonizing rhetoric of our political discourse. Management consultants advise corporate executives that compassion enhances workplace harmony, employee well-being, as well as the bottom line. Antibullying campaigners implore school boards to include compassion in their required curriculum.

This summons for compassion echoes from across the world's wisdom traditions as well. As Karen Armstrong, the noted scholar of religion, observes, teachers and guides from all faiths, all wisdom schools, and all spiritual traditions extol compassion as the truest mark of our humanity, the deepest essence of the transcendence interlaced with the universe, and the most promising path to peace on our planet.[2] The Charter for Compassion that Armstrong inaugurated has been signed by nearly one hundred thousand people of faith. It reminds us that some version of the Golden Rule is the ethical core of every religion.

Jewish rabbis and scholars, for example, consider the ethic of compassion the summative commandment of the Torah. This is witnessed to in the famous Talmudic tale in which a pagan approaches the great sage Hillel and promises to convert to Judaism if Hillel can recite the entire Torah while standing on one leg. Hillel, up to the task, responds simply, "What is hateful to yourself, do not do to another. That is the whole Torah. The rest is but commentary."[3]

The rest is but commentary for Buddhism as well. The four boundless attitudes that foster enlightenment are all facets of connective care: compassion, loving-kindness, joyful delight in another's delight, and the equanimity that extends such caring regard to all beings—animals and strangers, the loving and the difficult—with unwavering impartiality.[4] Indeed, when a disciple asked the Buddha, "Would it be true to say that part of our training is for love and compassion?" the Buddha succinctly responded, "No. *All* of our training is for love and compassion."[5]

Christian teachers also have admonished their followers to love not only their neighbor as themselves—to care for the suffering, the poor, and the outcast—but also more radically, to love their enemies as well—to forgive those who trespass against them, to bless those who curse them, and to return good to all, even those who do evil. Jesus compared God's compassion to the sun that shines on the just and the unjust alike. He summarized the essence of his spiritual path: Be all-inclusively compassionate, just as your Father in heaven is all-inclusively compassionate.[6] (See Matthew 5:48 and Luke 6:36.)

This radical ethic of compassion seems extraordinary to the point of being unattainable—or attainable only to the gifted few. Those few who embody compassion in the extreme seem saintly. An Amish community forgives a man who shot and killed their schoolgirls. A South African president invites his jailor of twenty-seven years to stand at his side during his inauguration. A Palestinian woman who has lost her son in a terrorist bombing takes in an Israeli boy and raises him as a Jew. A violated gardener befriends an angry boy and teaches him how to grow roses. These exemplars shimmer with the miraculous. Ordinary folk like us stand in awe, amazed and inspired.

We can also feel indicted and shamed by these examples. Genuine compassion is excruciatingly difficult. How do we refrain from doing what is hateful to another when someone treats us with hateful disdain? How do we care with unwavering impartiality when tension, exhaustion, and unending demands are unwavering burdens on our spirits? How do we love our enemies—a stepfather who abused us, for example—when their impassive nonrepentance renders mercy obscene and downright irresponsible? How do we love our enemies when, driven by perfectionism and our own castigation, our enemies are ourselves? How do we love our enemies when the people who most repel and infuriate us are our very own children, partners, or parents?

While spiritual teachers and advocates of the common good increasingly call for compassion, seldom does anyone explain precisely how to cultivate it.[7] In the absence of practical guidance, acting compassionately seems a near impossible ideal. Our angers, fears, drives, and aversions burn with primal power. Without a means to tend them, we either succumb to shame at our inevitable failures, or we suppress our repulsions, pretend we don't have them, and force a civility that rings hollow to both others and ourselves.

This is not compassion. Compassion is not about willing away unpleasant emotions and feigning politeness to those we secretly despise. Compassion is genuine loving regard that flows freely from the heart. Its path transforms perfectionist self-hatred into authentic, empathic self-compassion. It rekindles the care we truly feel for our loved ones and fosters a relationship in which we all feel heard. It tames the furies we feel toward an abuser and heeds our pleas for the protection, power, and personal dignity prerequisite for any possibility of truthful encounter and accountable reconnection. The path of compassion emboldens personhood. It restores our capacities to love others and ourselves with equal measure. It leads us back to our humanity.

This book describes how.

The Practice at the Heart of It All

The intricacies of *how* are encapsulated in the practice detailed throughout the rest of this book. Practicing compassion reconnects us to the sources of compassion that resuscitate and sustain the pulse of our spirits. It calms the difficult emotions, drives, and self-talk that tyrannize our interior worlds and transforms them into grounded, free, and empowered self-compassion. It restores our capacities for genuine compassion toward our loved ones, friends, and allies but also, more radically, toward our opponents, our enemies, people who trigger us, and people who threaten us. Lastly, practicing compassion discerns wise and restorative actions that care for the suffering, protect the vulnerable, and preserve the dignity of ourselves and others.

This practice—the Compassion Practice—unfolds into layers of intricacy and unveils subtle dynamics of deep transformative power. Its simplest form, however, has an elegant simplicity. The Compassion Practice invites us to

1. *Catch your breath* (Get grounded). Get some emotional and physical distance in whatever ways help you become centered and reconnected with the source of your vitality.

2. *Take your PULSE* (Cultivate compassion for yourself). Take a U-turn and connect empathically with the cry of your soul hidden within your emotions and impulses.

3. *Take the other's PULSE* (Cultivate compassion for another). Turn toward the other and connect empathically with the cry of the soul hidden within his or her emotions and behaviors.

4. *Decide what to do* (Discern compassionate action). Now grounded in compassion—both for yourself and the other—discern those actions that heal the suffering and nurture the flourishing of all parties involved and do them.

These deceptively simple moves hold the secrets to cultivating genuine compassion. They reconnect us to the sources of life and love; they kindle a healing care for ourselves; and they give rise to the loving regard that repairs our relationships. In short, the Compassion Practice restores the heartbeat of our humanity.

CATCH
YOUR
BREATH

Get grounded.

TAKE
YOUR
PULSE

*Cultivate compassion
for yourself.*

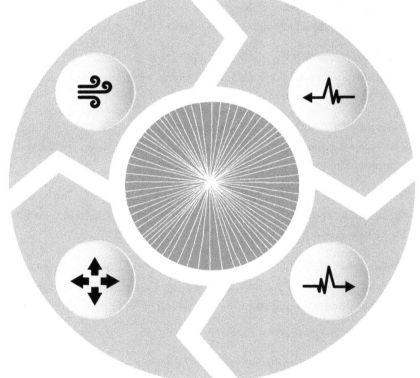

DECIDE
WHAT
TO DO

*Discern
compassionate action.*

TAKE
THE OTHER'S
PULSE

*Cultivate compassion
for another.*

Chapter 1

THE PULSE OF COMPASSION

An Overview of the Practice

In January of 1995, Azim Khamisa awakened to find a business card tucked in his door from the homicide division of the San Diego police department. Azim called the number on the card, and an officer shared with him the tragedy. Azim's only child, a twenty-year-old college student named Tariq, was delivering a pizza during the night in a neighborhood known for occasional gang violence. As Tariq sat in his car, another car pinned him from behind. Two teens got out. Tony Hicks, all of fourteen years old, was handed a gun by the older teen, the gang leader. Tony was ordered to take down the unknown deliveryman. Tony obeyed. He shot Tariq one time, the bullet piercing Tariq's heart. Within several minutes, Tariq suffocated in his own blood. The officer had come to inform Azim that his son was found dead at the scene.

In the months that followed, Azim struggled with rage, helplessness, despair, even thoughts of vengeance. A devout Muslim, he also struggled with the Islamic invitation to resist being consumed by hatred and to find a way to forgive even the unforgivable. He took care not to act out in his anger, but he didn't suppress it. He meditated prayerfully and sought therapy for his grief. Over time, the pain subsided, and Azim felt a sacred presence sustaining him. That sacred presence was expansive. It held him and his family. It held his slain son, Tariq. And it also held the boy so troubled that violence toward a stranger felt attractive.

Azim came to realize that there were victims on both sides of the gun. Not only was his son killed, but an African-American fourteen-year-old boy—raised fatherless in poverty and ubiquitous racism—was being tried as an adult then tossed away into a prison cell for the unforeseeable future. Azim decided that the cycle of despair and violence must come to an end. He quit his job and created a foundation, named after his son, dedicated to eradicating the conditions of youth violence and teaching young people a peacemaker's path of nonviolence, forgiveness, and restorative justice. He invited the teenaged killer's grandfather to join him. Then Azim visited Tony in prison.

Though he had already felt some forgiveness in his heart, Azim grew anxious as he waited in the jail's grated visiting booth. He was unsure what he would feel when his son's slayer sat across from him. He imagined looking into the gang member's eyes and seeing the face of a cold-blooded killer. He prayed for mercy. The boy entered the visiting booth, and Azim looked into Tony's eyes. He did not see a killer. He saw a terrified child, beaten down by a world stacked against him.

As Azim described it, he gazed straight into Tony's soul and saw the boy's humanity. In that moment of connection, both of their hearts broke open, and both hearts were touched by a sacred grace. Azim shared—without malice or accusation—the grief of losing a son. And he listened to Tony share the pain of growing up fatherless in a gang-ridden ghetto. He wept for Tony. Tony wept as well, expressing how sorry he was and how he ached for some way to make it up. Azim offered Tony a way. Indeed, he did more; he offered Tony a job. Upon his release from prison, Tony could work as an advocate against youth violence through the foundation named after the very boy Tony had killed.[1]

The Essential Components of Compassion

Azim Khamisa embodies—in a rather radical way—the essence of compassion. Though often less dramatic, we all know whispers of this same compassion. A mother sees a child ravaged by fever and cradles him in her soothing arms; a colleague loses her job and a coworker offers support; an earthquake or tsunami devastates a country and from around the world people are inspired to provide relief. However faintly, the pulse of compassion beats within us all.

The essence of this pulse is straightforward. Compassion is simply being moved in our depths by another's experience and responding in ways that intend either to ease the suffering or to promote the flourishing within that person. Metaphorically, compassion is a movement of the heart—the quiver we feel, for example, when we see someone in pain.[2] The compassionate heart is soft and tender. In contrast to the cold or hard heart unmoved by suffering, the compassionate heart beats freely, supple enough to take in another's pain and to respond with acts of kindness, goodwill, healing, and justice.

Azim Khamisa is an example. Softened by grief and broken by suffering, his heart is neither numb to the presence of his son's killer before him nor hardened with feelings of vengeance and bitterness. Rather, it is softened to receive Tony's tragic reality, to be moved to tender understanding and care, and to respond with forgiveness—an invitation to make amends and the promise of a future awaiting Tony's release. Azim's heart beats to the pulse of compassion.

Often we feel compassion naturally and with an elegant simplicity, like when a child notices a wounded puppy, is moved by its mournful eyes, and soothes it with a tender caress. Other times, like with Azim Khamisa, the process is agonizing and complex and requires a sustained commitment to our own healing and the spiritual practices that support it. Either way, this compassionate pulse, when examined more closely, has several essential components. Though sometimes implicit or so subtle as to seem instinctive, every experience of compassion involves the following six dimensions:

1. ***Paying attention*** (Contemplative awareness). A precondition for compassion is a particular way of seeing others. Usually when we relate to one another we do so through judgments and reactions that are conditioned by our own needs, desires, feelings, and sensitivities. We do not see other persons on their own terms; rather, we perceive them through the filtered lenses of our own agendas. I seldom see my son, Justin, for example, in the poignant particularity of his longings, fears, wounds, and delights. I usually see him as the forgetful college kid who neglects to pick up his dishes or the straight-A student about whom I like to brag to my colleagues. Either way, he becomes objectified through my own personal agenda, not a subject with depth and uniqueness.

Contemplative awareness, as Walter J. Burghardt classically defined it, entails "a long, loving look at the real."[3] We experience contemplative awareness through the nonreactive, nonprojective apprehension of others in the mystery of their uniqueness. Azim sees contemplatively not when Tony is demonized as a cold-blooded killer or even lauded as the trophy of a restorative justice program but when Azim pays attention to Tony, peers into his very soul, and glimpses the terrified boy in lockdown orange who longs for restoration. The recipient knows the difference between being seen and being objectified. Compassion engenders the sense of truly being seen without the distortional filter of another's judgments or agenda.

2. *Understanding empathically* (Empathic care). Compassion entails being moved by another's experience. In Pali, Arabic, Hebrew, and Greek, the etymological roots for the primary words translated as *compassion* are linked to a person's vital organs—specifically the womb, heart, belly, and bowels.[4] In essence, when we are moved to compassion, our depths are stirred—often viscerally. When Muhammad, for example, sees the plight of a widow or when Jesus surveys the pain of Jerusalem, they are gut-wrenched before the suffering, heartbroken, sickened to the stomach; and their womb-like cores contract. In contrast to the coldness and indifference of the unmoved, a compassionate person allows another's pain or joy to reverberate within his or her deepest core such that he or she is moved to pathos before the other's suffering or stirred to delight before the other's flourishing. A compassionate person understands, in his or her depths, the wounds, heartaches, and longings at the core of another person's behavior and experience.

Azim understands Tony's experience. When he sees into the soul of the boy who killed his son, Azim is moved by Tony's pain and feels understanding about the wounds and oppressions that gave rise to Tony's behavior. Again, the recipient knows the difference between someone who cares about his personal experience and someone who is inattentive or simply uncaring. In the language of attachment theory, the recipient feels "felt," they feel "got," they feel like someone gets what they feel to the point of reaching true understanding.[5]

3. ***Loving with connection*** (All-accepting presence). A nonjudgmental, all-embracing, infinitely loving quality resides at the core of compassion. Like the mother cradling her child, the womb-like love of compassion carries no hint of shame, critique, aversion, or belittlement. Rather, it wells up with a connective care that extends toward others like the soothing wash of the sunlight's warmth. As Azim sees and is moved by the broken boy before him, love expands within him and flows out of him to connect him to Tony, even through the bulletproof glass of a prison visiting room. In turn, when softened to receive it, Tony feels accepted, forgiven, and known. Azim's presence softens Tony until the young man is able to grieve in the face of the pain he has caused and ache to be restored to his own humanity.

4. ***Sensing the sacredness*** (Spiritual expansiveness). Compassion is a spiritual energy. When our hearts open to others' suffering and a sustaining love flows through us, the veil of the everyday world we live in is pierced and relativized: time seems to stop, errands lose their urgency, perennial irritations feel petty and frivolous. In those moments, our spirits expand—our capacity to care deepens, our understanding for the plight of another extends, and our patience can seem infinite. Grace abounds.

Some people experience these compassion-filled moments as holy. These moments are icons of a sacred energy, cosmic and benevolent. They are portals of presence that remind us that compassion flows not from our hearts alone but from the very texture of the universe. We are plugged into and instruments of a cosmic field of loving energy that reverberates throughout all time and space, carefully holds every scar and wound no matter how deep or brutal, and seeps through the open heart willing to be the instrument of care for another.

When Azim sees into Tony's soul, a hush descends upon them both. Ordinary time becomes sacred. Azim experiences his own spirit as a fuller and freer channel of a vast energy of love in which he too is held and healed. And Tony sees not only that Azim is holding him with healing care but also that Azim's heart beats with the love of the universe that holds and heals as well. For a moment, Azim and Tony are held together by an enduring energy that sustains them both. The cosmic sea of love has found a channel that pours into the arid soil of a maximum-security prison. And in those sacred waters, all wounds are healed.

5. *Embodying new life* (Desire for flourishing). Compassion not only grieves with the wounded in pain but also yearns for the transformation of suffering into joy. Compassion celebrates when new life is birthed and embodied. Like the womb that receives and incubates with protective care, holding others' pain brings about life. Genuine compassion is not limited to moments of suffering, offering an empathic connection only as long as others are in pain. Genuine compassion takes as much delight in others' flourishing as it feels pathos for their pain. Indeed, pathos, when soaked with compassionate care, gives rise to the yearning that wounded persons flourish with the fullness of life.

   Azim feels sorrow in the face of Tony's suffering, but that sorrow swells into the aching desire for Tony to know healing and step into wholeness. And should that day come when Tony walks free from prison, a compassionate Azim will be the first one to greet him and celebrate Tony's rehabilitation. Compassion's tears are sometimes from joy, and they flow freely when lives are healed.

6. *Act* (Restorative Action). The sentiment of compassion does not close in on itself. It does not soak in a moment of tender pathos then simply walk away. Compassion is responsive. It takes some step toward easing others' suffering and nurturing their flourishing. A mother cradling a sick child searches for medicine that will heal; television images of a hurricane's destruction give rise to relief trips delivering supplies and repairing the damage; Azim sees an imprisoned boy and is moved to participate in the boy's rehabilitation.

   Compassion includes restorative action. Without it, compassion degenerates into sentimentality—feeling bad for others' pain but ultimately abandoning them to fend for themselves. Compassion walks toward, not away. It sits with the grieving, companions the forlorn, and walks shoulder to shoulder with those on the road pushing toward liberation. As the Jewish rabbi Abraham Heschel remembered about his time with Martin Luther King Jr. at the Selma march in 1965, in the work of compassion, there comes a time when we must pray with our legs.

These six dimensions compose the essential PULSE of compassion. In short, we define compassion as:

P—*Paying attention.* Perceiving another's experience with a nonjudgmental, nonreactive clarity.

U—*Understanding empathically.* Being moved by the sometimes hidden suffering within that person.

L—*Loving with connection.* Being filled with and extending an all-embracing care.

S—*Sensing the sacredness.* Recognizing and savoring the cosmic expanse of compassion that holds and heals all wounds.

E—*Embodying new life.* Yearning for the restorative flourishing to be birthed within another.

ACT—Then from the *PULSE* of this compassionate connection, we respond with tangible acts of healing, kindness, and care.

Azim Khamisa exemplified this. His heart beats to the pulse of compassion. Perceiving a tragically broken boy, he is moved by that boy's pain—so moved that he offers his own hand in transforming that pain into redemption.

Compassion May Require Cultivation

Many times our impulses to act compassionately come easily and naturally, like a child's tending for a bird with a broken wing. When whole and vital, our hearts beat with care and connection. Often, however, our lives are driven by much less sympathetic impulses. The pulse of our spirit can accelerate with busyness or hyper-reactivity. It can shut down and become dull with numbness or fatigue. It might beat erratically in cycles of rage and withdrawal or compulsion and shame. Sometimes compassion requires cultivation—the pulse of our lives needs to be tended and restored to the tender heartbeat of care.

Within the messiness of our lives, the Compassion Practice offers us a way to resuscitate and sustain our capacities for care and connection. It distills and synthesizes the principles and processes of cultivating compassion into four rhythmic movements. Of course, in the midst of our daily routines, if our hearts feel open, steady, and soft, the only practice we need is to act naturally—the suffering of others will move us; their joys will delight us; and connections will feel free, generous, and life-sustaining.

The need for a practice emerges when our hearts feel hard, cold, reactive, or depleted—a shopper dominates the express lane with a basket full of groceries and we burn with impatience and indignation; a loved one needs a shoulder to cry on, and we sigh with burden and fatigue; a tragedy strikes our family, and we are mired in a pit of outrage and pain. We need a practice that restores us to the pulse of our humanity when compassion seems elusive or even repugnant.

When we find ourselves disconnected from our natural capacities for care and connection, the Compassion Practice invites us to

1. *Catch your breath* (Get grounded). Our native wisdom is revealing. Whenever someone is seriously agitated, we instinctively say, "Take a deep breath." Likewise, when we are swept up in a current of emotions, passions, impulses, and drives that distort our capacities to care, our first move is to find solid ground. Acting out at the mercy of the drives and passions of our inner world only wreaks havoc for others and for us. We need to secure some distance—emotionally and, if necessary, physically—that allows our emotions to settle. Taking a time-out, walking outdoors, going on a retreat, finding a moment to ourselves or with God, or simply catching our breath solidifies our footing until the ground feels solid, safe, or perhaps sacred enough to engage the situation more clearly. This "moment" may need to last for a season. As would any of us, Azim Khamisa required ample space for healing before compassionate forgiveness could seem anything but offensive.

Catching our breath also entails returning to the sources of life and love that renew and sustain us. The springs of compassion flow from the abundance of love within us. We can only give of that which we have received. When we feel depleted or disconnected, our invitation is to return to the well and to drink deeply once more from the waters of compassion extended to us. In doing so, we remember the truth of who we are—beloved in our core—and how we are sustained by a sacred reality whose loving currents are the renewing source from which genuine compassion is cultivated.

2. ***Take your PULSE*** (Cultivate compassion for yourself). When we feel disconnected from our compassionate nature, our pulse beats erratically— gripped perhaps by repulsion, fear, envy—or grows dim with numbness or fatigue. The invitation, once grounded, is to take a "U-turn," to look inward, and to recalibrate our pulse to the steady heartbeat of humanity.[6] When we are agitated, reactive, or depleted, our inner world is in pain and in need. Ignoring the state of our soul and pressing to cultivate compassion for another is not only counterproductive but also a form of interior violence. It dismisses the needs and suffering that are crying out from within us. Forcing an open heart toward others while closing our own hearts to ourselves is as internally contradictory as screaming our way into silence, straining our way into relaxation, or battling our way into inner peace. The cry within us will only intensify and demand our attention in other ways, such as compassion fatigue, an intractable resentment, or a chronic knot in our neck. In the early days of his grief, Azim wisely heeded the impulse that it was too soon to face his son's killer. He needed to turn inward; he had healing to do and personal power to restore.

Self-compassion restores us to the steady heartbeat of our humanity. As we turn inward, we extend to ourselves the same compassion we would extend to others. Following the essential components of compassion, this essentially entails taking our own PULSE.

P—*Paying attention.* Cultivate a nonjudgmental, nonreactive awareness of whatever agitation is present within you.

U—*Understanding empathically.* Listen for and be moved by the suffering hidden within the cry of this agitation—the fear, longing, or aching wound in need of tending.

L—*Loving with connection.* As you are moved by the suffering within you, extend tender care toward the need or wound that presents itself.

S—*Sensing the sacredness.* Recognize and savor the cosmic expanse of compassion that holds and heals every suffering within you.

E—*Embodying new life.* Notice the gifts and qualities of restored humanity that are being birthed within you.

In taking our PULSE, we not only relax the reactivities, repulsions, fears, and drives that distort our natural humanity but also tend to the wounds and needs hidden within them. In so doing, we are restored to our selves—selves that are naturally compassionate.

3. *Take the other's PULSE* (Cultivate compassion for another). Once our hearts are steady enough to be open to empathic connection with others— this may take time—we can cultivate genuine compassion for others. We do so, as we did with ourselves, by connecting with the PULSE of humanity beating within them.

P—*Paying attention.* Cultivate a nonjudgmental, nonreactive awareness of what the person is doing and how he or she is doing it.

U—*Understanding empathically.* Listen for and be moved by the suffering hidden within the cry of his or her emotions or behavior—the fear, longing, or aching wound in need of care.

L—*Loving with connection.* As the suffering within the other person moves you, extend care toward the need or wound that surfaces.

S—*Sensing the sacredness.* Recognize and savor the cosmic expanse of compassion that holds and heals every wound within him or her.

E—*Embodying new life.* Notice the gifts and qualities of restored humanity that are being birthed within the person and yearn for his or her flourishing.

This pulse of humanity beats, however dimly, within all of us. No matter how distorted and beaten down we may become, an abiding capacity for care and connection remains alive within us. Azim discovered it in a hardened boy who killed at age fourteen. Many of the persons we encounter routinely, however, have not had their humanity all but obliterated. The people we more commonly engage are like ourselves— momentarily mired in the compulsions, fears, and sensitivities we acquire over a lifetime. Nevertheless, as long as our hearts are beating, the pulse of our humanity lives. Connecting with this pulse within others unlocks our genuine compassion, and such compassion has the power to soften even the most hardened of hearts.

4. **Decide what to do** (Discern compassionate action). As previously mentioned, compassion includes restorative action. Our cultivation of compassion is not complete when feelings of warm regard are experienced either toward ourselves or others. We must act out our

compassion in ways that ease suffering and promote the flourishing of others. Such acts include consoling the grief-stricken, tending the wounded, and befriending those who feel forsaken. Yet actions that are genuinely compassionate often require careful discernment. What does compassion look like, for example, when the wound caused by another is still fresh or when an offender refuses to curb his or her violence and remains unrepentant?

Compassionate action must serve and sustain our own healing and restoration. Cultivating compassion is not an invitation to minimize our needs for healing and wholeness, to silence our voices, to abandon our personal power, or to lose ourselves in endless caretaking to the point of depletion and fatigue. Compassion yearns for the flourishing of *all* life, including our own. Our capacity for genuine compassion flows out of the strength and fullness of our vitality. Whenever we are disconnected from our capacities for compassion, wounds within remain in need of our attention.

Compassionate action also invites the restoration of others. In the case of an offense against us, such restoration demands accountability. Compassion is not sentimental. Violent actions create wounds, and perpetrators must be held responsible. Azim had compassion for Tony and then offered him a chance to heal and rehabilitate. Their relationship was restored only because Tony was willing to take responsibility for his actions, show remorse, commit to his own recovery, and, to the best of his ability, make amends by devoting his life to the prevention of further teenage violence. Azim's compassion paved the way, but the restoration of Tony's humanity and the possibility of reconciliation required Tony to walk the road.

And what if Tony had refused, turned defiant, or remained unrepentant? Azim's compassion could still hold strong in the midst of the horrors perpetrated by Tony and Tony's defiance. However, Azim's compassion would carry a resolve: A dangerous man should be sequestered, and his unchecked violence must be prevented from affecting other families. Compassion does not endorse the perpetuation of violation. But it does seek to see the ember of humanity in even the most violent of offenders. With grief for tragedy and an assertive determination to safeguard life, compassion limits violence even as it appeals to the perpetrator's humanity though his or her pulse may be buried.

These essential movements—the core rhythms that restore us to our compassionate essence—make up the Compassion Practice, as seen in the graphic on page 20. Layers of intricacy are yet to be detailed, as are various capacities that enhance the process's effectiveness. But for all the complexities hidden within, the fundamental movement of compassion remains elegantly simple. Whenever you feel disconnected from your compassionate core: *Catch your breath. Take your PULSE. Take the other's PULSE. Then, and only then, decide what to do and do it.*

Coda

To this day, Azim Khamisa works with young people in communities ravaged by gang violence. He also works tirelessly for Tony Hicks's release from prison. Tony has earned advanced degrees, written hundreds of letters to marginalized youth much like him, and tirelessly advocated for alternatives to violence. Together, Azim and Tony bear testimony that compassion is possible even in the most tragic of circumstances. In situations where victims lie on both sides of a gun, Azim and Tony point to the hope that healing is possible. The compassion they embody is not limited to saints and exemplars. It is available to us all. Such compassion meets us precisely where we are and unveils the love we long for—a love that restores the heartbeat of our humanity.

Chapter 2

Catching Our Breath

Getting Grounded in the Soil of Compassion

In 1962 Rev. Dr. Martin Luther King Jr. attended a weeklong Christian leadership conference in Birmingham, Alabama. At the time, Birmingham was the most thoroughly segregated city in America. Schools, swimming pools, public parks and bathrooms, drinking fountains, fitting rooms, and even checkout stands in grocery stores were designated with the placards reading *Colored* or *Whites Only*. Indeed, the crusade to preserve segregation was so extreme that a children's book was banned in the libraries, stores, and public schools for showing black and white sheep together on the same cover.

Tensions were high. Thaddeus Eugene "Bull" Connor, the Commissioner of Public Safety, dispersed a rally of schoolchildren by knocking them off their feet with fire hoses and then unleashing his attack dogs on them. African-Americans were routinely raped, lynched, castrated, and spat upon. Churches were vandalized. Civic leaders were beaten. The neighborhood where black activists lived was bombed so many times the newspapers dubbed it "Dynamite Hill."

Into this war zone of racial tension King came to preach his gospel of love and to encourage the people to begin nonviolent campaigns of boycotting stores, staging sit-ins at restaurants, and marching through the streets in peaceful protest against the indignities of segregation and racism.

During his visit, King addressed a crowd of people in attendance at
a church. The place was packed. People filled the pews and the aisles, the
window alcoves and balconies. Even the parking lot was fitted with speakers for the overflowing crowd. As King began his closing remarks, a white
man stood up and walked toward him. King was weary. His house had been
bombed three times already. He had received death threats in the mail for
years. He had been stabbed in the chest while delivering a sermon in Har-
lem. But not until the man was directly in front of him did King see the
hatred in his eyes. The man lunged at King, knocked him backward, and
beat him on the face and back. The church erupted. A mob swarmed around
King, grabbed the attacker, and herded him toward the door. Cries rang
out, "Kill the bastard! Lynch him! Beat him to a bloody pulp!" And into the
midst of all the cacophonous chaos, one voice boomed through the room:
"Stop! Leave him alone."

The church fell silent. The voice they heard was Martin Luther King
Jr.'s, his face transcendently calm. King walked over to the man, put his arm
around the assailant's shoulder, and looked around the crowd.

"What would you like to do?" King asked the crowd. "Kill him? That
isn't our movement. Would you like to use Molotov cocktails? That is not our
movement. I'll tell you what our movement is. It's to understand him. Yes,
even him. It's to ask what it would be like if you were taught since you were a
child, since you were baby enough to crawl, that the Negro is a *thing*! If you
were taught from your parents, from your teachers, from even your ministers
and the people sitting next to you in church that it isn't wrong to hate, what
would you be then? That's what this movement is. It's to reveal these people
to themselves."[1]

––––––––––––

Through an extraordinary act of compassionate intervention, Martin Luther
King Jr. saved a man from certain beating. He also prevented an escalation of violence that likely would have sabotaged a nonviolent campaign
in Birmingham before it even started. King's intervention was only possible, however, because of his capacity to remain grounded even in extremely
reactive circumstances. Many issues could have provoked a punitive or
retaliatory reaction from King: the arousal of fear when approached with

menace, previous trauma in King's life, the instinctive rush of adrenaline and fury when physically assaulted. Instead, King retained his footing on solid ground and called a halt to the violence.

King maintained his internal equilibrium in three ways. First, King literally and figuratively caught his breath. In the chaotic swirl of escalating conditions, the emotions and passions of the moment did not hijack King. He took a breath. He found some way to relax despite his instinctive response to protect himself when threatened. In resisting to act impulsively, King remained well-grounded. And from such internal stability, he could assess the situation calmly, firmly, and with clarity.

Second, King's capacity to respond to an assailant immediately with compassion reveals that he was well-grounded in the truth of his own belovedness. As I've mentioned before, we can only give of that which we have received. We can only treat another with dignity when we know our own dignity. We can only extend compassion to others when compassion has been extended to us. From a variety of sources—possibly his parents and family, his mentors and professors, his faith community, his prayer life—King internalized a profound sense of his own worth and his place within the Beloved Community for which he so fervently advocated. His internal reservoirs of love and compassion were already filled. His value did not depend upon the esteem of others. His sense of self-worth was so secure that it intuitively repelled the pounding lies of degradation in the fists of a racist attacker. Becoming grounded includes remembering our truth—we bear dignity as members of the Beloved Community. And no one can beat that truth out of us.

Third, King's capacity to extend radical compassion drew from a deeper well than his own. His commitment to nonviolent love as a means of transforming the hearts of his opponents was grounded in a sacred reality. King embraced the man who attacked him not merely out of his own compassion but out of the sacred compassion in which all things are held and interconnected. King called this sacred reality God. And King believed even his attacker was one of God's children. Even his attacker was a member of the Beloved Community. For it is a community in which all people belong by virtue of common ancestry in the Divine. King and his assailant were brothers. And both of them were held in love. Both of them were eternally embraced in the arms of God's compassion. For King, becoming grounded entailed sinking his roots deeply in the sacred soil that reveres and sustains all life.

We may seldom find ourselves in conditions as extreme as King did in Birmingham. We are, however, routinely knocked from our compassionate centers. We spend vast portions of every day reacting to persons and situations instead of responding in deliberate and connective ways. We are driven, rather unconsciously, by our fears, angers, anxieties, despairs, and the passions that feed our addictive compulsions to work, eat, stay busy, or check out in front of the TV. A grounded internal stability often eludes us. In the cascading currents of busyness and reactivity, our capacities for care and connection can thoroughly erode.

When we find ourselves knocked off-center, we need a path that stabilizes and restores us. In the Compassion Practice, the first step of this path invites us to simply find solid ground. Like the three aspects King embodied in Birmingham, this ground solidifies underneath us when we catch our breath within the fury of reactivity and impulsiveness, when we remember and are emboldened in the truth of our belovedness, and when we root ourselves deeply in the loving essence of the universe—the spiritual source, however we know it, in which all of creation is held in the Beloved Community that welcomes us all.

Getting Grounded When Knocked Off-Center

Nick, a friend of mine, described a peace vigil he once attended. After the invasion of Iraq, in the wake of 9/11, a Quaker group organized a silent witness for peace at a busy intersection in his town. Nick, a longtime practitioner and teacher of contemplative practice, arrived a few moments after the vigil began. The leader, a gentle elderly woman, approached him to share the parameters. Her lifelong commitment to Quaker activism nurtured a spirit of radiant calm that informed the design of the vigil. They gathered, she explained, to create an oasis of peace within the fever of war. Nothing more. They would merely be a silent presence of care. Respect and courtesy would be extended to all who passed. But no words were to be uttered. They would embody peace not debate it. Peace speaks for itself.

The woman cautioned Nick that this could be difficult—people might gesture, honk their horns, or shout their dissent. Nick assured her that as a teacher of contemplative practice he knew how to be silent. He scrawled a sign that read *Peace For Our Children* and took his place on the edge of the sidewalk.

Within moments, right in front of him, a pickup truck stopped at a red light. The windows of the truck were rolled down, and talk radio blared from the speakers. The man inside fumed at the traffic, glared all around, saw Nick, and spat out, "Your children would be dead if we lived in Iraq."

Nick, seasoned contemplative that he is, spat right back, "Your children will be dead if we keep bombing innocent people."

"Don't talk about my children!" the man shot back.

"Don't talk about mine!" my friend rejoined. "I want peace for them all!"

"I'll show you peace!"

"Show me! I'm right here!"

A gentle arm wrapped around my friend's shoulder. He heard these words whispered in his ear: "That's okay. Just take a deep breath. Why don't we go for a little walk."

Nick and the elderly Quaker woman did walk. As the light turned green, the truck pulled away. And the peace vigil settled once more into silence.

In an instant, reactive emotions can erupt from within us and hijack our consciousness. It happens to us all. Even to contemplative practitioners. To be sure, anger can hijack us—a boss trashes the work we have labored on for weeks, a group cuts into the line we've stood in for hours, a pickup driver diminishes our children while we are standing at a rally—and fury ignites within us instantly. Other emotions hijack us as well. We have a presentation to make, and anxiety burns through our bellies. Our child takes an overnight trip, and fear all but paralyzes us. We hear the name of a lover who has left us, and grief stabs us with rejection.

When hijacked by our emotions, we are gripped in their powers. Like being swept downstream in cascading currents, we are carried away by the activated energy coursing through us. At such times, no separation exists between our impulses and our behaviors. We get mad, we yell. We are fearful, we cower. We see the ice cream, we binge. We feel anxiety, we shut down. In brief, an impulse gets activated, and we act out in its power.

What we need when we are activated like this is to wedge some space between our emotions and our behaviors, between our impulses and our actions. We need to find solid ground within the raging rapids of reactivity or the slow-moving drift of unconscious routine—a place to stabilize ourselves within the possessive current and to secure a vantage point from which we can lift our heads and assess our situations.

Such solid ground is *awareness*. Becoming *aware* of our emotions, drives, and internal states instead of acting unconsciously consumed by their power creates a space between impulse and behavior. For example, if my friend had noticed with nonreactive awareness the fury within him that a truck driver's words triggered, a space of awareness could have interrupted the impulse to yell back in defense. Within that space, we can settle ourselves and then assess a more deliberate reply. This is the difference between *reacting* to life's circumstances and *responding* with grounded, reflective self-awareness.

How, when activated, do we create this space for self-awareness? Our native wisdom is an instructive starting point: Take a deep breath. Regulating our breathing—slowing it down when accelerated through reactivity or deepening it when shortened through tension and anxiety—grounds us in the moment. It actually restores us physiologically. Regulated breathing activates the relaxation systems in our bodies. It stabilizes our oxygen mixture, steadies a rapid heartbeat, calms tensed muscles, invigorates endorphins, and dissipates toxic chemicals released in our bodies. Our breathing literally recalibrates our bodies.[2]

The world's spiritual traditions recognize the power of our breath to ground us. Nearly every contemplative and cultural path to spiritual development begins with attention to our breathing. This is true for meditation. And it is true in the moments when we are activated by destabilizing impulses. Breathing is the most basic and efficient spiritual practice to restore and sustain a grounded posture. Anthony de Mello, an Indian Jesuit priest, puts it succinctly: "Your breathing is your greatest friend. Return to it in all your troubles and you will find comfort and guidance."[3] And the miracle of the body is that this friend is ever present, ever available. Our groundedness, quite simply, is a single breath away.

Sometimes a few moments of regulated breathing are enough to dispel an agitated state. Other times, we need to widen the gap between arousal and response—the emotion is too intense, the impulse to react goes too deep, the situation's complexities cloud our vision. At such times, we need more space in order to emerge from the rapids of reactivity and solidify our footing on the banks of grounded perspective. Catching our breath means taking a break. We need a time-out. We need to let settle the turmoil within. We can do this in multiple ways.

Change your location. Go for a walk, spend time in nature, find a quiet place to sit, take a drive, or take refuge in a sacred site—a chapel, mosque, temple, or monastery.

Engage your body. Do yoga, get a massage, take a bath, go for a run, ride a bike, throw clay, make music, dance, or draw.

Connect with a trusted person. Visit your therapist or spiritual director, talk with a friend, confide in a loved one, consult a mentor or spiritual teacher, seek counsel from a priest, pastor, rabbi, or imam.

Perform a spiritual practice. Pray, meditate, journal, repeat a mantra, walk a labyrinth, go on a retreat.

Such grounding activities give us space. They increase the distance between arousal and response. They bring calm to the agitated currents swirling within us. And with calm comes clarity. When a snow globe, shaken into a flurry of glitter, is stilled long enough for the glitter to settle, the dimensions of the landscape within become clear. Likewise, in taking the time to ground ourselves, our agitation can relax, and the underlying dynamics within our emotions, drives, and behaviors can come more fully into view. We may not be completely restored to our compassionate center, but we can at least see the tensions that need to be tended. We will have settled onto the stabilized ground from which compassion, both for ourselves and others, can be intentionally cultivated. The bottom line is, when triggered, don't just do something, sit there.

Remembering Ourselves as Beloved

Once we secure our footing on solid ground, we can take stock of the condition of our soul's terrain. Is the ground of our interior stability rich and fertile, the air crisp and fresh? Or is the ground arid and cracked, the air dirty and dry? Our capacities for compassion flow from the wellsprings of love within us. When we feel vital and valued, compassion seems ample and effortless. When we are harried and depleted, compassion feels burdensome and laborious. The well-loved child offers care freely; the deprived child becomes cold and withdrawn. We can only give from that which we have. We can only love with the love from within us.

The wellsprings of love and compassion within us can be replenished. We are, each one of us, wired for attachment. As much as food and water, we need love and care to survive. Without them, our spirits would wither. Our will to live would burn out entirely. That we function at all bears testimony that somewhere along the way we have been seen and validated. Persons in our lives recognized us for who we are. They affirmed our worth and beheld our beauty. They accepted us unconditionally. And the compassion they bestowed upon us kept alive the pulse of our humanity.

Some years ago, a college student boarded a bus heading home for spring break. The bus nearly full, he sat down next to a man staring out the window. The man was middle-aged, dressed in denim, and bore the hardened look of someone haunted by a life he would rather soon forget. The man was not interested in small talk. He was lost in himself. He simply gazed at the passing cornfields and farmhouses as the bus rolled along the two-lane country roads.

A couple of hours into the ride, the middle-aged man grew agitated. He stared down at the floor, only casting quick glances out the window as if daring not to look too long. The college student asked if the man was okay. The man regarded him, glanced once more out the window, and felt desperate enough to share his tale.

"Twenty years ago," the man confessed, "I killed a man. I was boozin' it up, got inside a car, never saw the guy just crossing the street. I've been in prison all these years just thinking about it. I felt so ashamed that I sent a letter to my folks. Told them that I knew I wasn't any good, and that I was in prison, but I didn't tell them where. As far as they were concerned, they should count me dead. I haven't seen or heard from them ever since.

"I got paroled a couple days back. Didn't have a place to go really. So I wrote my folks. I told them I was getting out. I know I've brought nothing but shame to them and our family. But if they would have me, I told them I would love to come home. I understand if they don't want me back. So I've made it easy on them. In our front yard is this big, old oak tree. The bus drives right by our house on its way into town. If they will have me, all they need to do is tie a yellow ribbon around that tree. If it's there, I'll get off the bus at town and come on home. If it's not there, I'll get it. I'll just stay on the bus. And they don't ever have to lay eyes on me again.

"The thing is, now that we're getting close, I'm not sure I can bear to look. If that oak tree is bare, why, I don't know what I'll do."

The middle-aged man started to look out the window then stopped himself, staring back down at the floor instead. Then an idea came to him.

"Say," he asked the student, "would you mind looking for me? I'll just look the other way, and you can let me know."

The student agreed. They swapped seats. The student scouted. The man stared down at the floor. House after house passed by. Tree after tree was barren of ribbons. The bus neared the town. Then, with a shout, the student saw it.

"Oh my God, you *have* to see this!"

The man dared to look. The bus was passing his childhood home. A giant oak tree stood sentry in the yard. The tree did not bear a *single* yellow ribbon; it boasted *hundreds* of them. Flapping in the breeze from every branch of the tree, an explosion of yellow ribbons proclaimed to the world, *Our boy is coming home. And we cannot wait to embrace him.*

People who extend compassion to us are guardians of our soul. John Makran-sky calls them benefactors, emissaries of love in our lives.[4] These are people who see us, understand us, value us, and celebrate our homecomings. They offer us the inestimable gift of revealing to us the truth of who we are—we are worthy of love even in our shame; we are held with love even when we forget it; our beauty is beheld even when we feel blemished; though our jour-neys leave us broken and burdened, we are and remain thoroughly beloved.

Such emissaries of love sustain our spirit. Receiving their love replen-ishes the reservoirs out of which our own compassion might flow toward others. We receive their love by taking the time to remember them, acknowledge their gift, and soak in and savor the care they so graciously extend to us. We can do this in a variety of ways. Makransky suggests the Buddhist practice of meditating on their loving presences. We can savor their presences in other ways, as well—writing about their acts of care, telling their stories to others, placing their pictures in sacred places, expressing gratitude directly to them, or simply lingering in the grace of their memory. Whatever the method, drinking deeply from these restor-ative waters fills the well of compassion within us. To give love, we have to receive love. In receiving more fully the love given to us, we have more from which to give to others.

Some spiritual writers remind us that whispers of kindness and com-passion are extended to us throughout each day—the courtesy of a stranger holding a door for our passing, the smile of a friend from across the room, the hand that holds ours when our spirits are down, the loved one who cares how our day has unfolded. Often, these register but for a moment and then flow right on past us. Practices like the Ignatian daily awareness examen or the Buddhist meditation on receiving love help us notice and savor these whispers of compassion.[5] These practices recognize that the soil of our soul grows all the more fertile as these showers of kindness soak deeply within and collect into the pools of our interior reserves.

We can also be our own guardians of compassion. Self-care is painfully neglected in our world, and our souls and loved ones pay the price. Heightened reactivity is a symptom of a soul depleted and undernourished. Recognizing when our souls are weary and replenishing them restores our capacities for staying grounded within the cascading crosscurrents of our lives.

We rekindle our interior vitality through those activities that leave us refreshed and energized, more alive and available—shooting hoops, going skiing, rock climbing, writing a poem, preparing a feast, dancing, painting, planting a garden, playing the guitar, playing with children, spending time with the love of our lives, and so forth. Cultivating our vitality solidifies our center. When fully alive, we are less reactive. Paradoxically, self-care increases our care for others. Loved and alive, we have love to lavish on those around us.

Knowing Ourselves as Beloved

For many spiritual traditions, breath is intimately connected with the sacred and sustaining life force of the universe. *Chi* in Taoism, *Prana* in Hinduism, *Lung* in Tibetan Buddhism—all refer both to our literal breath and, more profoundly, to the animating life energy of every living thing. In Hebrew (*ruach*), Arabic (*rouh*), Greek (*pneuma*), and Latin (*spiritus*), the words for *breath* are synonymous not only with the human spirit but also with the Divine spirit.

Jewish scripture particularly underscores this. Our breath, the Hebrew Bible suggests, flows from the very breath of God. Humanity is created when God breathes the sacred breath of life into the mud-formed being of the first human. And God's continuous breathing sustains our lives each moment. If God's breath were held, humanity would perish.[6] Indeed, some observe that the Hebrew letters for God's name, YHWH, are associated with the pattern of breathing—*Yod* (inhale), *Heh* (pause), *Vav* (exhale), *Heh* (pause).[7] If spoken aloud, God's name would sound like breath. Breathing itself is a prayer. It is a prayer we have been praying since the moment of birth.

Catching our breath, then, deepens our connection with the sacred source of life, the vital spiritual energy that sustains and restores all living things. This life-bestowing energy permeates our existence and envelops our world. It is the sustaining presence in which we live and move and have our being. As Anthony de Mello suggests, "The atmosphere is charged with

God's presence. Inhale God as you inhale air."[8] Or as the mystic poet Kabir sees it, we are as immersed within God as fish within the sea.[9]

This sacred, sustaining energy is not neutral toward us. Connecting with it and resting in its currents is intrinsically healing and revitalizing. It is an animating force—a spirit—that has a quality to it, the quality of life and love. This sacred presence has a pulse—it beats to the pulse of compassion.[10]

Spiritual traditions affirm this. As Karen Armstrong observes, "All faiths insist that compassion . . . brings us into relation with the transcendence we call God, Brahmin, Nirvana, or Dao."[11] Compassion is the essence of this sacred transcendence. In its presence, we feel known, held, loved, and celebrated. When anthropomorphized, it bears a face not of judgment, aloofness, or punishing strictness but of infinite understanding, radical acceptance, and extravagant care.

This sacred compassion is the face of the Jewish Shekinah whose tears weep for the children slaughtered in captivity. It is the embrace Jesus describes of an ecstatic father welcoming a prodigal son home. It is the grieving pathos of the Mater Dolorosa—Mary holding in her lap the slain body of her son. It is Kwan Yin, whose name means, "One who hears the cries of the world," and whose thousand arms, tending all who need aid, are revered by Buddhist and Taoist alike.[12]

The sacred breath that sustains all life does so willingly, benevolently, generously, and delightedly. And in the same way that our bodies without breath would deteriorate and perish, so too without a sustaining connection with the sacred energy of love, our spirits would wither and die. Without compassion, the soul decays.

———————

During seminary, I served as a student intern at a church. Early one Saturday morning, I met a young boy, maybe twelve years old, sent by his mother to fetch a pastor. The night before, his brother had shot himself. I went with the boy. For several hours, I sat with his mother in wordless grief. Then as I was leaving, the boy, Joey, begged a ride back to the church. We sat in the parking lot, the morning still grey, as Joey laid bare some of his pain.

It became quite clear that Danny, sixteen years old, was not only Joey's big brother but also Joey's only loving refuge in a house with a violent and addicted father and a mother so depressed she could not leave her bed to prepare meals for her sons. Joey spoke of many cherished memories of his brother. Then he shared words that still stay with me: "I want to ask you something," he said. "Something happened a few months back that I have been wondering about. Dad came home really ripped, ready to beat up anybody in his sight. Danny and I ran out of the house and down the hill. We got ourselves a couple of sodas at the store and hung out at the park. It was nighttime, and the two of us just sat there, waiting until we thought it was okay to go back. We didn't talk much. We just looked up at the stars.

"All of a sudden, this flying star just shot by, and the two of us started wishing upon this star." And Joey described a litany of wishes—two boys, back and forth, Danny, the older, leading; Joey, the younger, responding in kind.

"I wish I could play baseball like Willie Mays."

"I wish I could pitch like Juan Marichal."

"I wish I had a brand new car."

"I wish I had a ten-speed bike."

"I wish Regina had the hots for me."

"I wish Suzie would leave me alone."

"I wish Dad would stop hitting everybody."

"I wish Dad didn't drink so much."

"I wish that Mom were happy."

"I wish that she would cook us dinner."

"I wish that Mom didn't need me so much."

"I wish that she would talk to me."

"I wish that Dad were dead."

"I wish that Mom would clean his clock."

"I wish that I were a long, long way from here," Danny mused absently.

As Joey described it, he did not offer a wish in reply to that one of Danny's. It was as if Danny really were a long, long way from there. But then Danny continued. "You know what I wish?" he asked. "I wish that I could fly. And if I could fly, I wish that I could fly right up into heaven. And I would fly right up to where God is sitting, and do you know what I wish? I wish that I could look straight into his face, and he would look back at me and smile." Then he took his empty soda bottle, threw it against a concrete wall, and spewed, "But the bastard would probably turn his back."

Joey turned to me on that grey Saturday morning and asked, "What I want to know is, was Danny right? I mean, I know we can't, but if we could. If we could fly and see the face of God, would God smile at us or just turn his back?"

———————

Joey gives voice to a longing that echoes from the deepest shadows of our souls. If we could stand face-to-face with the essence of the universe, would we see something cold and capricious or welcoming and benevolent? For Joey—and ultimately for Danny as well—it was a question of life or death. They knew a soul cannot long survive a certainty that God's face would scorn and disown it.

Joey's question haunts us as well. In regions so dark we seldom plumb them, a chilling uncertainty wails. At the rock bottom of life and eternity, in the presence of the sacred foundations of the universe, is our pain seen and held, are our cries heard? Are we, though bruised and battered, truly beheld as beloved?

The questions echo deeply. Deeper still is the truth.

In the bedrock of our soul we know. We have glimpsed this face of the universe. And with eyes filled with tears for the world, it is a face of infinite compassion.

In spectacular, unforgettable, mundane, and profoundly tender ways the sacred compassion that sustains our world has touched our lives. We have glimpsed it—in the eyes of a loved one who sees our shame and treasures us anyway, in the kindness extended to us and our families in times of immobilizing grief, in moments of mystical oneness with the beauty of creation, in the laughter of children, in the falling of snow, in the glistening of stars, in the innocence of a newborn's eyes. In each of our lives, moments of heightened connection amaze us with wonder and envelop us with wordless grace. These moments are sacred. They are portals of presence, icons through which we catch sight of the benevolent essence of the universe. And when we are immersed in such moments, we sense that we are not alone in the world. We are beloved. We are held not just in the care of our companions but also in the infinite love of the universe. This is the truth. This is the ground of transcendent compassion. Standing firm on this sacred rock, we know precisely how to answer the question of a haunted and lonely boy.

Joey, if you know nothing else, know this: Wherever you find yourself before the face of God—whether in heaven, on earth, or in the living hell of a violent home—God will be smiling toward you with radiant delight, so pleased and proud to see you.

———

Our capacities for compassion are deepened when we stay grounded in the sacred truth of our belovedness. So often we forget. We start believing the lies that we are not worthy of love. We seek the source of our value in our work, wealth, physical appearance, and in others while deep within, the longing lingers. We long for the face of the universe to turn toward us with care.

The path of compassion invites us to remember that our belovedness is as secure as the air we breathe. It is the ground on which we have our being. The face is smiling as we speak. Remembering, reconnecting with, and rooting ourselves deeply in the loving essence of the universe reminds us of the truth of our sacred belovedness. We deepen our connection with this compassionate presence in various ways—prayer, meditation, solitude, retreat, worship, ritual, fellowship, and community. Many reconnect with this sacred presence by remembering and savoring the sacred moments that have graced them throughout the course of their lives.

Regardless of religious practice, the invitation is the same. Return to the ground of infinite compassion. Behold your face held as beloved. Breathe this love into every fiber of your being. And leave replenished, loved and alive, as a bearer of love for our world.

The Sacred Source of Compassion

When I was a graduate student in spirituality, I met a man who knew how to ground himself in the sacred source of compassion. I was in need of spiritual replenishment, so I paid a visit to the local monastery set at the edge of town. It was early when I drove through the gates. Instantly, I entered a world both still and mystical. I drove along the road and parked beside a '64 Rambler. I found the chapel and entered through the front door. The altar was already set—candles lit, a draped plate of bread, a filled chalice of wine. Weekday Eucharist was about to commence. I stepped into the sanctuary. And that is where I first met Harry.

Harry was an elderly gentleman sitting alone about halfway toward the front. He wore clothes that looked like they had been bought at a thrift store—a tattered tweed jacket, a wrinkled white shirt, a clip-on tie inside a V-neck sweater. Most distinctive, however, was this stranger's posture: he had turned around and was beaming in my direction. It was as if he knew me, as if he was waiting for me. Like he was the host of this party, I was the guest of honor, and he was so glad I had finally arrived.

Having no idea who he was, I simply smiled back, sat on the chapel's opposite side, and ignored him during Eucharist. When Mass was over, he grabbed my arm, and we chatted as we walked toward our cars. So began our daily ritual.

I learned his name, Harry, and that he was eighty-three years old and a retired telephone repairman. He and his wife raised two boys on a working-class salary. He was proud of them both—proud that they went to college and both became doctors. Harry lived alone. Some fifteen years earlier, his wife had died after forty-seven years of marriage. Every day after Mass, Harry would drive to the retirement home on the far side of town where he would spend the morning talking sports and playing checkers, listening to Sinatra and gossiping with the women there. He never went emptyhanded; he always brought donuts, turnovers, or bear claw pastries—unless it was a special occasion, in which case he would bring his legendary seven-layer cake. Rumor had it nobody could bake a cake like Harry's seven-layered masterpiece. Harry, quite simply, was one of the most charming people I had ever met.

One spring morning, I asked him a question. "Harry," I began, "every day I come to Mass, you're already here. You're always smiling and engaged. It's clear how important this is to you. What about the Eucharist is so meaningful that you make it the center of every day?"

Harry cocked his head, leaned forward on his cane, and stared into the distance. "I don't know," he mused after a spell, "I guess it just feels right somehow." And then, almost as if he were changing the subject, he said, "Say, did I ever tell you about our fortieth wedding anniversary? Man, was that something else. The missus and me, we'd been married forty years, and we were busting to do something special. The boys were away at college, so it was just the two of us. We dug out our best clothes from the closet, got all dolled up, and drove an hour all the way to the Jersey Shore looking to find the best restaurant around. No Denny's for us, no sir. We wanted something classy. And as it turned out, we found something even classier than we knew existed: a restaurant that's only open for dinner. Can you imagine? Denny's is open twenty-four hours a day—you can get a Grand Slam for breakfast at two in the morning. Not this place. Only open for dinner. Now that's classy.

"But we didn't know that at the time. We just drove up in front of this fancy-looking place on the ocean and walked in. There was this man all dressed up in a tuxedo by the door, and he asks if he can help us. I say, 'Sure, we've come here for dinner. We'd like a table for two.'

"He says, 'That's fine, the only problem is, it's a quarter to six, and we're not open yet.'

"'You're kidding,' I say. 'You're a restaurant, right?'

"'That we are, sir,' he says. 'But here, we only serve dinner.'

"I'm thinking to myself, *Now this is a classy place.* So I say, 'Well, okay, is there someplace we could sit and have a glass of wine? You see, today's our fortieth wedding anniversary, and we've come to celebrate.'

"And just about then, the owner of the restaurant walks by, overhears us, and says, 'You two been married for forty years?'

"'Sure have,' I say.

"'Get outta here, forty years today?'

"'Yes sir. And ready to do forty more.'

"'Well, come on in,' he says. He takes off our coats, and in we go.

"Man, you should have seen this place. It was like walking into paradise. All the tables had white cloths and crystal wine glasses and four or five forks and spoons lined up next to the china. They had plants coming out of the ceiling and a grand piano so shiny you could see your reflection in it. They even had a sculpture made of *ice.* I'm telling you, this place was classy.

The owner, he takes us to this big round table by the window—the best seats in the house—helps us into our chairs, and says he'll be right back. Well, me and the missus are still figuring out what all the forks are for when he comes back with the guy in the tuxedo, a bottle of champagne, and four glasses.

"'This is on the house,' the owner says, 'We're going to have a toast. Tonight, we celebrate forty years of wedded bliss.' Well, he's working the cork off the bottle when one of the waiters walks by. 'What's going on?' he says. 'We aren't even open yet.'

"The owner says, 'These two have been married for forty years.'

"'Get outta here,' the waiter replies, 'really?

"'Yeah,' the owner says, 'go get yourself a glass.' He runs off and another waiter walks by.

"'What's going on? We aren't even open yet.'

"'These two have been married for forty years.'

"'Get outta here, really?'

"'Yeah, go get yourself a glass.' He runs off and a waitress walks by.

"'What's going on? We're not even open yet.'

"'These two have been married for forty years.'

"'Get outta here, really?'

"'Yeah, go get yourself a glass.' Then a busboy comes, a few more waitresses, and more waiters too with more glasses and more champagne until there's so much commotion going on they hear us way back in the kitchen. This guy with a chef's hat leans out the door and hollers, 'What's going on out there? We're not even open yet.'

"'These two have been married for forty years,' everyone replies.

"'Get outta here, really?'

"'Yeah, go get yourself a glass. Get the other cooks. Get everyone who's around. We're celebrating forty years of wedded bliss, and everybody's part of the toast,' the owner says.

"The next thing you know, there's about thirty people standing around our table, some of them wearing tuxedos, some of them in jeans and aprons, all of them with a glass in the air as happy for us as if we were family. And you know what, they didn't even know our names. I tell you what, that was one classy place."

I stood there watching him. For a moment, he had come alive, radiant in this memory when strangers gathered around a table to celebrate love and marriage. All I could think to say was something pretty silly. "Gee, Harry, those are the moments that really warm your heart, aren't they?"

He paused for a bit, still recalling the sacred waters of that toast. Then he looked up at me and said, "Warm your heart? No. Those are the moments that keep me alive." Then after a few moments, he spoke again. "Tell me something," he said. "You're a seminary student. Do you think heaven will be like that?"

This time I knew just what to say. "Harry," I said, "I think heaven is going to be *exactly* like that."

"I hope so," he said. "I hope so." And with that, he settled into his car and drove across town to share a few hours with a different group of strangers whose lives he felt moved to toast.

––––––––

Harry knows. He has glimpsed the truth of who he is. A simple telephone repairman, he is welcomed at the table with patrons of classy restaurants. His forty-year, working-class love is worthy of champagne with strangers. Staying grounded in this truth, his wells of compassion for others are abundant and overflowing. He becomes the gracious host to spiritually depleted seminary students and elderly residents of a retirement facility, welcoming others to the table of life where they too belong.

Harry replenishes these springs each morning through his spiritual community's connection with this sacred source. He remembers the truth of his and others' belovedness in a Catholic monastery's early morning quiet, in the stories of grace he shares with a companion, and in the bread and wine of the eucharistic meal laid out for all to partake.

For Harry, this is only appropriate. For him, that moment of grace in a Jersey Shore restaurant was a window into the sacred compassion that holds and sustains all life. Harry had a peek at heaven. A wedding toast shared amongst strangers was a glimpse of the feast of life to come. It is a feast where all are invited and welcomed—racist assailants and civil rights leaders, hotheaded truck drivers and reactive peace activists, ex-cons, abused boys, aproned dishwashers, tuxedoed maître d's, and telephone repairmen.

It is the feast of the Beloved Community. It is the feast that celebrates the sacred love in which all lives are worthy of toasting. This is the ground that feeds compassion. This is the ground that holds us all. This is the ground that keeps us and the world alive.

GETTING GROUNDED

Connecting with Your Breath

1. ***Find a rhythm of breathing.*** Determine a comfortable posture—either sitting or lying on your back—then take a deep breath, inhaling from and into the deepest part of your belly. It may help to place your hand on your diaphragm and notice your stomach extending as you fill it with air. Hold the breath in for a couple of beats then exhale as much air from your body as possible. Inhale again breathing air into a deeper part of your belly, hold it a moment, then exhale once more. After several such breaths, each one slightly deeper than the one before, allow yourself to settle into a gentle rhythm of deep breathing that nurtures an interior silence.

2. ***Connect with the breath's sacred energy.*** If it feels helpful, imagine that you are breathing in with each inhale a sacred presence or energy—*Chi, Prana,* Spirit, for example—and with each exhale imagine that you are releasing anything that disconnects you from that sacred reality. As you sense what this sacred energy feels like, it may help to imagine that reality as a color, a light, or a sensation such as warmth, peacefulness, or compassion. Allow each inhale to deepen the sense of the sacred energy permeating your body and soul.

3. ***Breathe the sacred energy throughout your body.*** As you continue to breathe, become aware of your body one part at a time. Breathe sacred energy into that part with each inhale and allow the energy to soothe that part in whatever way feels right. Begin with the top of your head, breathing in sacred energy down the length of your spine. Next, become aware of the

center of your forehead, and breathe in a sense of sacred presence that fills your skull and brain. Continue with your eyes, your ears, your mouth and jaw, your neck and throat, your shoulders, your arms, your hands, your heart, your belly, your lower back, your groin, your thighs, your calves and ankles, and finally your feet. Notice if any part of your body remains in need of this sacred energy for whatever reason and breathe in this energy around that part, continuing to do so until you feel settled in an abiding sense of sacred connection.

4. *Rest in contemplative presence.* Allow yourself to rest in this sense of inner stillness anchored by the steady rhythm of your continued breathing. When you become distracted by a thought, a feeling, or a bodily sensation, allow the distraction into your awareness and breathe this sacred energy upon it until it relaxes, settles, or dissipates.

5. *Return.* When you are ready to emerge from this meditative space, invite this sacred energy to continue to sustain your breathing. Whenever you feel reactive, impulsive, or otherwise disconnected from your center, pause for a moment and allow a few deep breaths to return you to a sense of settled presence.[13]

IN THE MOMENT

Over the course of your day, break the ongoing stream of your natural reactions to the world by simply taking a few breaths and noticing them. Breathing is a foundational grounding exercise—one that is foundational to all the practices that follow. Pause and notice your breathing especially when you find yourself particularly triggered in any way.

GETTING GROUNDED

Remembering Sacred Moments

1. Take several deep breaths and then settle into an interior silence.

2. Like thumbing through a photo album of your life, become aware of various moments in your life or week that felt sacred or expansive to you—moments of life, love, joy, wonder, or heightened connection. These may be intense and unforgettable moments or simple and mundane whispers of presence and connection. Of the various moments that come to you, allow one to emerge as the focus for the rest of this exercise.

3. Remember this moment by returning to it in your imagination.

   > Recall what was going on in your life at the time, where you were, and who accompanied you.

   > Reexperience the sensory details of the moment—the sights, sounds, smells, tastes, and bodily sensations.

   > Remember what seemed sacred or expansive about the moment and how this expansive presence felt.

4. Allow the presence of this sacred expansiveness to swell once more within you. For as long as it feels right, rest in and savor this presence. Think of a symbol that embodies the essence of this presence—a healing light perhaps, a divine figure, or a warm embrace.

5. In preparing to conclude this practice, discern if there is an invitation from the sacred for how you might allow the grace of this prayer to extend into your daily life.

In the Moment

Find a tangible object or symbol that reminds you of one of your sacred moments. Carry this in your pocket or on a chain around your neck. Throughout your day, take a breath, remember this object, and be aware that this same sacred expansiveness is with you at all times.

Chapter 3

Taking Our PULSE

Cultivating Compassion for Ourselves

At eight months old, my son, Justin, took in everything. He loved to perch himself on the edge of his stroller, like a baby bird looking out from a nest, and scan every movement that played out before him.

One day, he was posed this way while I walked him through a St. Louis mall. As the rest of the family shopped, I meandered with Justin among the folks crowding the mall's corridors and courtyards. Tired of walking, I leaned against a concrete planter and pushed him back and forth while Justin observed everything from his stroller perch.

While lingering there, I noticed a woman, perhaps retirement age, coming down the corridor toward us. Obviously upset, she defiantly plowed through the crowd, shopping bag clutched in one hand, a handbag in the other. People scurried out of her way as she barreled along. I was sure a straggler could get mown down in her stride. I had no idea where she was heading or by whom she had been wronged, but I feared for the unsuspecting soul who dared get in her way.

What I did not notice was that Justin was watching her too. His wide-eyed look was befuddled, and he gazed straight at her as she beelined through the crowd. As she got close, her head twitching in agitated fury, she did not break stride, but her scowling eyes glared sideways and locked onto Justin's. Justin's eyes, still wide with wonder, looked unblinkingly back into hers. And then he did the most amazing thing. He smiled. And with his smile, I watched as all of the hardness of that woman simply melted away. She let out a sigh, put down her bags, sank to her knees, and for several minutes, gave herself to giggling play. She tickled his toes; Justin grabbed for her glasses. Both of them cooing, ahhing, and glowing in delight at the unconditional beauty they beheld in each other. They were radiant. They were glorious. They were restored into the wonder of what humanity looks like when fully alive and flowing with love.

After several minutes, the woman looked up and noticed me. She mused a moment then offered simply, "God bless him. And God bless you too." And with that gesture of goodwill, she grabbed her bags and walked away.

When we are most human, most alive and connected, our hearts beat to the pulse of compassion. Sometimes this is as instinctive as a child smiling spontaneously at a burdened and ill-humored shopper or as abounding as a rejuvenated woman blessing a baby and the parent behind the stroller as well. All too often, however, our lives are driven by impulses far less tender. A neighbor boasts of an Ivy-League-bound grandchild, and we seethe with annoyance and inferiority. A loved one comes down with a case of bronchitis, and we groan with resentment and exhaustion. A salesclerk with attitude treats us discourteously, and we become the enraged shopper fuming through the mall. Compassion often requires cultivation. We need a path that leads us to the face of love that restores us to ourselves.

The great secret of compassion is that this face is hidden within us.

Our Compassionate Core

The cultivation of compassion is really a process of recovery—of retrieving an inherent capacity that has become, either in the moment or over time, buried and obscured. We know how to care. We are wired for connection. We are born to love and to be loved. In truth, our deepest core is naturally compassionate. Spiritual traditions affirm this. Buddhists believe that Buddha's nature of love and compassion dwells within the essence of every sentient being. Jews and Christians hold that each person is created in the image of God—a God of infinite and extravagant compassion. Sufi poets refer to the "Beloved Lover" that inhabits every soul. An essence of compassion dwells deep within us. It is our true self—our true face, if you will. We are most fully human when we live from this essence. We are most fully our true selves when we most fully love.

The woman in the mall demonstrates this idea. When she is restored to herself, the burdens of fury having fallen away, care and connection flow freely and abundantly. She does not need to coax herself to be compassionate through willpower or spiritual practice. Once the hardness of her distress eases and washes away, care and connection are simply present. She returns to the truth of who she is. Her face beams once more. She is herself again, an inherently compassionate self.

This is true to our experiences as well. We all have moments when we see persons, perhaps children, hurting, lost, or in tears, and our hearts spontaneously go out to them. We are moved by their pain, and we yearn to ease their suffering. Or we see radiant and alive persons—teenagers dancing, playing music, scoring goals on a soccer field—and, taken by their joy, we delight in their beauty and bliss. In such moments, something feels right inside of us; we feel in harmony with our human essence. We might even say to ourselves, *Yes, this is me. I'm being true to who I really am.* Conversely, should we rush by the whimpering child in our haste to meet our days' demands or disparage the teens indulging in activities that bring them joy, something feels off inside us. Our actions feel uncharacteristic, and in hindsight we might think, *I wasn't really myself that day.*

Psychologists such as Carl Jung and Richard Schwartz and mystics in the tradition of Thomas Merton refer to this enduring essence of humanity within us as the "Self."[1] Our Self is our true nature and the ground of our being. It is the pulse of love ever beating at the center of who we are. Moments of care and connection allow our true Self to shine. Such moments, even in as mundane a place as a St. Louis mall, can seem transcendent. The dullness and hardness and disconnection that pervade our chronic busyness dissipate. We experience a heightened awareness, a grounded stability, an abundance of love and goodwill. The face of our humanity beams unmarred like a woman beholding a smiling baby.

This compassionate core dwells intact within every living soul. Our outer shells may be numbed by indifference, hardened into coldness, or distorted by fear and fury, but the unblemished face of our true Self resides within each one of us. Like a pilot light of the spirit, our capacity to love lingers in the soul. As long as our hearts are beating, an impulse of care remains alive within us, a care both restorative and sacred. As the Quaker mystic George Fox observes, "There is that of God in everyone."

The enduring presence of a compassionate core—a Self that loves both freely and abundantly—suggests that the cultivation of compassion does not entail compelling a loving regard from ourselves. Rather, it is a process of clearing away the obstacles that prevent the free flow of our natural capacity to care. The act of cultivating compassion is similar to the legend about the famous Renaissance sculptor Michelangelo. As he hauled a slab of marble through the marketplace, a villager yelled out, "Michelangelo, what are you doing with that giant rock?" To which the sculptor responded, "You see a giant rock; I see an angel inside yearning to be free." As we relax the fears, drives, passions, and hostilities that obstruct compassionate connection, our loving essence organically emerges from within. The face of our true Self reappears. As one Eastern proverb observes, "When the eye is unobstructed, the result is sight; when the ear is unobstructed, the result is hearing; when the mind is unobstructed, the result is wisdom; and of course when the heart is unobstructed, the result is love."[2]

Two Ways of Being in the World

But what about those tenacious obstacles? The affirmation that our truest essence is compassion—that care and connection flow naturally from us—does beg the question: What do we do when we are not feeling particularly compassionate? Truthfully we spend vast portions of our lives disconnected from our compassionate core. Reactive emotions consume us—anger, fear, despair, and disgust. Internal voices harass us—voices of self-loathing, perfectionism, blame, or judgment. Behavioral impulses drive us to work, play, stay busy, or simply numb ourselves. If a true Self lies deep within us as an enduring capacity for grounded compassion, a self that feels false and disharmonious remains at the forefront of many of our everyday encounters.

Spiritual writers have referred to this variously as being enslaved to our lower nature, consumed by the passions of the flesh, captive to a false consciousness or false self-system, and driven by the needs of the ego. Regardless of its characterization, we experience two qualitatively different ways of being in the world. We have moments when we feel grounded, centered, patient, and compassionate and other moments when we feel off-center, disconnected, moody, or impulsive. These latter moments are states in which some psychic energy—an emotion, thought, fantasy, or behavioral impulse (what Ignatius of Loyola termed "interior movements" and what Richard Schwartz refers to as "Parts" of us)—has come with such force we are enmeshed in its agenda and carried away by its power. These states can endure. We may spend an entire day, for example, driven by the compulsion to work. Or they can come with the fury of a flash flood—a flare of anger at the sight of an offensive bumper sticker.

We classify interior movements into five categories:

Emotions (for example, anger, fear, lust, jealousy, and despair),

Internal monologues and inner voices (for example, voices of self-criticism, self-hatred, judgment, and perfectionism),

Impulses and desires (for example, to work, eat, have sex, veg out, and surf the Internet),

Images, daydreams, and fantasies (for example, daydreaming about a vacation while at work or fantasizing about getting revenge on someone who has hurt us),

Bodily sensations (for example, a dread in the pit of the stomach when going to a meeting with a supervisor, a heartache when thinking of a lost loved one, or a tensing of the body when considering the number of bills still to be paid).

These interior movements alienate us from our compassionate core. Indeed, they displace us from the grounded agency of feeling in charge of our lives. It is as if they emerge, either instantaneously or in a slow advance, and take over the driver's seat of our consciousness. We are wheeled around at the mercy of their whims. We feel things we would rather not feel. We behave in ways we later regret. Compulsions that we cannot resist take over and we find ourselves doing things we know are not constructive for ourselves or for the people around us.

These states feel all-encompassing. While we are enmeshed in them, the entirety of our personhood seems defined by the interior movements that have captured us. It feels as if we *are* the anger that consumes us; we *are* our addiction to food; we *are* the incompetent frauds our self-hatred rebukes us to be. These are illusions. Our emotions, impulses, and inner voices are not who we are in our cores. They are charges of energy that have surfaced from the depths and hijacked our consciousness, at least for the moment. They mar the face of our true humanity. They disconnect us from the ground of our true Self. They are distortions of our sacred essence. Even so, they are here. And when they possess us, our compassionate Self seems like a long lost acquaintance whose face we can no longer remember.

An example may be illustrative. Home from college, my son asks to borrow the car while I am at the office. This is fine, I assure him, as long as he picks me up on time—the previous summer he was perpetually late. After several sessions of spiritual direction, I'm feeling rather grounded and centered. I leave my office, greet some colleagues, and arrive at the curb precisely at six. Sure enough, my son is not there. Five minutes go by and then ten without so much as a phone call. The irritation begins to boil within me. Before I know it, I want to scream. I want to scold him, shake him, and shame him into respecting my very simple request. My heart no longer beats with the pulse of compassion; instead it is pounding with fury and outrage.

In an instant, an interior movement has ignited and taken over the wheel of my consciousness. I'm not driving the bus of my being anymore— anger is. And anger drives like a madman. When an interior movement appears within us, we usually do one of two things—we either act out or we resist it. *Acting out* involves unconsciously surrendering to the possessive power of the movement's energy and demands—I might seethe and pace the sidewalk, play and replay an internal monologue (*I was absolutely clear what I needed from him! This happens every time! When is he going to respect someone else's needs?*), or launch an attack upon his arrival, fume in the car, and drill him about the repercussions of his obvious and chronic lack of consideration. Unconsciously acting out is a state of being enslaved to the interior movement taking over the driver's seat of our souls. Clearly disconnected from my grounded and compassionate core, I have *become* the movement itself. I *am* my rage. The energy of my fury has effectively eclipsed the core Self of care and connection buried within me.

Resistance entails subjugating our reactivity or repelling it by sheer force of will. I might insist to myself that I'm really not upset at all, berate myself that I wouldn't be upset if I were more spiritually evolved (*You are a teacher of compassion after all!*), or perhaps simply minimize my feelings (*You really shouldn't be so impatient.*) and shrug off my anger so as not to ruin my evening. Resistance is a way of fighting the initial interior movement. In fact, it is a form of internal warfare. Rooted in shame, self-judgment, or discomfort that the movement is there at all, resistance seeks to banish it, discourage it, or overpower it so as to be rid of it altogether. This too is a state of disconnection from our grounded and compassionate Self. It is equally a form of captivity to an alienating interior movement—it is enmeshment, not in the anger itself, but in the repelling energy that resists and reacts to the anger.

Both strategies are unsatisfying and counterproductive. Acting out, far from resolving the conflict in question only intensifies the disconnection I feel with my son and poisons my soul with toxicity in the process. And resistance is like trying to submerge a buoy underwater—the triggered emotion remains fully charged and keeps popping to the surface with dogged persistence. Both are forms of internal slavery, either to the psychic energy itself or to the counterenergy determined to diminish the first. Neither brings healing. Neither resolves the issue. And neither restores us to our compassionate essence.

Taking the U-Turn

The way of compassion suggests a radical and counterintuitive alternative to acting out or resisting internal movements. Acting out and resistance are both ways of maintaining focus on the external world—on the persons causing our distress or on the situations that provoke our reactions. We think that if we can change the circumstances, it would change the way that we feel. For example, *If Justin is on time,* I rationalize, *I would never become angry. If he did not make me feel angry,* I continue, *I would not beat myself up with shame.* Instead of focusing our attention outward, compassion invites us to turn inward, to take a U-turn, and to attend to the movements activated within ourselves. This is akin to the teaching of Jesus—when we see a speck in the eye of another, we should first tend to the logs in our own eyes. (See Matthew 7:3-5 and Luke 6:41-42.) It even echoes the airline instruction to secure our own oxygen masks before attending to other passengers.

The psychological observation behind this invitation is twofold. First, it recognizes that we can maintain a grounded Self-awareness free from enmeshment within *any* interior movement. When crosscurrents of the emotions and impulses that drive us take over—sometimes through acting out, sometimes resisting, sometimes in a high-pitched battle that goes back and forth—we are not in our right minds. We have lost our footing on the ground of our being. Our core Self has been displaced from the driver's seat of our lives. This is unfortunate because our core Self serves as our greatest resource. It anchors us at the center of the storm in our cacophonous inner world. It serves as the peaceful reprieve from the unceasing war between acting out and resistance. It frees us from the tyranny of our internal impulsiveness.

Spiritual teachers and explorers of the psyche have recognized this ground of Self-presence that is free from enmeshment within our emotions, thoughts, and impulses. Hindus refer to it as Atman, ego psychologists as the Observing Ego, Buddhists as the Witness when in a state of mindfulness, Thomas Merton as the Inner I, Quakers as the Inner Light, others as the seat of consciousness, the seat of the soul, or the seat of divine indwelling.

However named, the core Self resides in a qualitatively different sphere of consciousness than absorption within an interior movement. When grounded in the Self, we experience a state of *detachment* because we are detached from the possessive clutch of any internal movement.[3] It is also a state of *awareness* in which we are *aware* of movements within us without losing ourselves within them—the difference between "My heart is really pounding with fury" and the unconscious enmeshment of "I am so furious right now I could hit something."[4] We also can describe it as a state of *nonreactive, nonjudgmental openness,* of not resisting the presence of interior movements but allowing them to gently float on the untroubled surface of our awareness like cloud reflections mirrored on a glassy, still pond. The U-turn invites us to cultivate this interior space of grounded and detached Self-awareness. This open awareness cannot be defined as full-blown compassion, but it serves as a return to the ground of our Self whose abundant capacities for compassion wait only to be tapped.

The second psychological observation behind the invitation to take a U-turn is that our discordant interior movements are rooted more within ourselves than in the world outside. Our reactions to the world primarily concern us. The fury at Justin, for example, that thunders through me shows signs of a sensitivity within myself and not a violation by him so inherently egregious it defies the reach of even a saint's compassion. We see that this sensitivity is mostly my own issue because countless others respond to tardiness with patience and understanding, perhaps even savoring the few moments of solitude. Yet I find such patience elusive. Further, the severity of my reaction tells me something—a mere ten minutes, a "speck" of tardiness, so to speak, causes a "log's" worth of indignation within me. Clearly something in my own soul requires tending and restoring. The invitation toward compassionate Self-restoration asks that I calm and recalibrate the erratic pulse to which my own heart races and only then may I tend to the situation at hand from a more grounded and centered posture.

This insight—that our reactions to the world are primarily based in us— ultimately liberates us. The power to claim and retain our own humanity lies in us and not in others. Our responses to the world do not depend upon what other people do to us even when they treat us in harmful and provocative ways. We can cultivate a grounded Self-presence so secure that like birds resting on electrical wires, thousands of volts of charged energy can course through us without eroding our strength and dignity. No one has the power to rob us of our Selfhood. Others can demean us, but they cannot dehumanize us. Our humanity belongs to each of us. And the path to claiming it requires compassionate attention to the turbulence within us.

Interior Movements as Cries for Compassion

Another radical realization textures the invitation to take the U-turn and tend the erratic movements within us, one with life-transforming potential. Every interior movement we experience—every emotional fluttering, mental monologue, imaginative fantasy, or behavioral impulse—is rooted in a cry of pain or a need straining to be heard. All interior movements bid for life. They attempt to protect us from a threat, to claim power and vitality, and to secure the love and connection on which our flourishing depends. An interior movement may become extreme, destructive, or relentless when something essential for our survival is threatened and demands our attention. Such movements are fighting for our lives in the only way they know how. As Richard Schwartz observes, every movement within us means well and is rooted in some positive intention.[5] Or as Marshall Rosenberg says of extreme emotions, every tenacious interior movement is but the tragic cry of an unmet need.[6] Here are a few examples: pangs of jealousy at a colleague's new book may be the frustrated groans of the book within us aching to be birthed, an impulse to surf the Internet for hours may be the exhausted plea for some centered downtime, or a voice of relentless self-castigation may be the scream of terror at being rejected if we are unable to reach perfection.

Each one of these energies—jealousy, rage, compulsivity, self-castigation—wreaks havoc within our inner worlds and are but the wail of an unsoothed *fear* (of violation or attack, for example), an unsatisfied *longing* (for rest and renewal, perhaps), an *aching wound* still bruised (such as scars of abandonment or rejection), or a *gift* obstructed and undeveloped crying out to be owned and nurtured (cultivating self-expression, for example, or claiming our personal voice). To be sure, their pleas can be painfully clumsy and tragically desperate. They come out as, "Why do her books always get so much press?" or "I'm never going to be good enough." The hidden cry underneath, however, says, *I'm in pain. Please, someone, see me.* Our interior movements bid for healing, wholeness, and integration. They serve as reliable barometers of what our souls need to survive and flourish in the world. They yearn to be heard, held, and healed. They are not our enemies; they are battered guides pointing the way to life.

This is revolutionary. Normally we war with our inner movements. When not carried away by their possessive power, we judge them as bad or destructive and manage them through power of will or distraction. I feel shame for my anger at Justin and siphon it off by running a few miles or bingeing on Häagen-Dazs ice cream. Or I fear my anger's destructive power and push it away through interior scolding. In reality, this only intensifies my internal conflict. Emotions and drives elude any attempt to be handled. I might secure a short-term reprieve, but my anger returns in full force the next time Justin is ten minutes late—or if not Justin, a colleague, a partner, a delayed airplane. Like a child who screams louder when ignored, these interior energies become more severe when their cry is unheard and their suffering is dismissed. They long not for subjugation but for compassionate care.

This recognition opens the door for a radically new relationship with the movements that rage within our inner worlds. Instead of fighting them with strategies of resistance, taking the U-turn invites us to listen with care to the cry of pain hidden within them. It invites us to do for ourselves what we would do for another. If friends came to us unnerved by persons who had left them waiting or beating themselves up after sniping at their children, we would listen with care and understanding. In the same way, this is an opportunity to listen to the agitated cries within us. And when we do so, something happens. The suffering within those cries surfaces. We are moved. Compassion fills us up and flows from within. The face of care that is our core emerges once more. And remarkably, as we extend this care to the turmoil within us, the interior stirrings relax, their deep needs make themselves known, and, in the attentive gaze of our compassion, they are healed and made whole.

This is genuine Self-compassion. Compassion flows from our true Self, and we extend that compassion to the cries of suffering clamoring within our own souls. The path of the U-turn restores the Self; it restores the heartbeat of our compassion.

Taking Our PULSE

How then do we cultivate such Self-compassion? How might I, for example, recalibrate the racing pulse of my anger at Justin to the pulse of compassion and turn my attention to myself? The first step of the Compassion Practice invites us to catch our breath. We need to find some way to interrupt the rush of reactivity and regain some emotional grounding—taking a walk, playing music, meditating, connecting with a confidant. Then, using my example, instead of scheming how to change my son or even forcing a compassion for him that I do not feel, the second step of the Compassion Practice invites me to cast my gaze inward and take my PULSE.

Following the five components of compassion outlined earlier, I would start by *paying attention.* Paying attention involves cultivating a nonjudgmental, nonreactive awareness of whatever movement has been activated within us. Such awareness does not remain enmeshed in the movement or enmeshed in any judgmental, reactive, or resistant countermovement. It simply acknowledges that one or more movements are present. This awareness settles us in the ground of Self-presence that is genuinely open to the movement and curious about why this movement is within us at all.

Grounded Self-awareness can be extended to any interior movement— emotions like rage, lust, depression, and fear; internal voices of self-laceration and judgment; impulses to binge, work, commit acts of violence; fantasies of love, escape, or revenge. This Self-awareness trusts that every movement within us is, at its root, a bid for life, a cry for care. And it holds all movements with a radical acceptance and welcoming spirit that is open to understanding the cry hidden within it. It is the posture described in Rumi's poem "The Guest House" that opens the door of our Self-awareness and welcomes any interior visitor that comes, for each "has been sent as a guide from beyond."[7] If, in the course of paying attention, we do not feel open to a movement that is present—if, for example, we find ourselves judging it, handling it, afraid of it, or analyzing it—then we are enmeshed in another interior movement. So we cultivate a nonreactive, nonjudgmental welcoming awareness of *that* additional guest. And we continue until we ease into the space of genuine openness.

In the case of my reaction to Justin's tardiness, I notice that fury is present within me. Without fanning its flames or fighting its energy, I can simply be aware that this emotion is present. I would also notice that shame, self-judgment, and an impulse to self-medicate on ice cream are activated within me as well. I would welcome them all to the guesthouse of my awareness. Each emotion means well; all are burdened with pain. I invite them to relax now that they have my attention. As I open myself to these emotions, I ease once more into the presence of my Self. I am in my right mind again. And from this posture of restored Self-presence, genuine understanding and compassionate connection are possible. Now I am in a place to listen more deeply to the cry of the fury within me.

Once we are grounded in Self-presence and are truly open to the interior movement, we then seek to *understand empathically* the suffering hidden within it. The movement itself is a cry—something vital to our thriving feels threatened or at stake. Like an indicator light on a dashboard, the interior movement signals that something needs our attention. Or alternatively, the movement is like the waving flag of a person in distress, frantic that his or her need be seen and tended. We cultivate empathic understanding through listening deeply to the movement until the source of its distress makes itself known. The distress within the frantic FLAG of an activated interior movement is rooted in one or more of the following:

F—*Fear.* The movement is terrified of an imminent danger—perhaps rejection, ridicule, violation, attack—and mobilizes to protect us from the threat.

L—*Longing.* The movement yearns for something essential to our flourishing—for renewal, freedom, love, or life.

A—*Aching wound.* Pain from the past still stings and bleeds and when triggered in the present, cries out to be held and healed. These wounds could come from shame, abuse, abandonment, or neglect.

G—*Gifts obstructed.* The movement holds the burgeoning seed of a talent or a personal capacity that has been denied and buried and is bursting to be claimed and nurtured into flourishing—the gift, perhaps, of our voice, power, tenderness, or art.

When we hear the source of the cry within the interior movement, something shifts inside of us. We are moved. An understanding dawns; we think, *No wonder I respond, act, or feel this way.* We finally understand, we soften, and compassion rises from within.

What might surface as I listen deeply to the cry within the waving FLAG of my fury at Justin? I would hold the fury in my curious gaze and ask myself: What does my fury *fear*? For what does it *long*? What *aching wound* is tender and stung? What *gift* or strength has been stifled or discouraged and pleads to be claimed and nurtured?

Perhaps I would sense that my fury is rooted in a deep terror of being forgotten—ten minutes of tardiness feels like a lifetime of being abandoned and left alone. It may help to imagine my fury as a child or to allow a memory to materialize. One comes. The pain feels like that of a wounded boy—me at eleven years old—shivering in the cold because his preoccupied mother forgot to retrieve him from a swim meet in the next town over. I see the boy trembling in the dark, his back against the wall of a deserted recreation center. Beholding that boy moves me. No wonder I recoil when I feel forgotten. A neglected young boy has ached for years for someone to soothe his aloneness in the world and to heal the ancient terror that he really deserved nothing more. I get it now. Understanding dissolves the fury and comes from the true face of my Self.

Understanding gives rise to *loving with connection.* Like the mother cradling her crying child, we offer care. We reassure the fears that terrorize from within. We hear the longings and heed their needs. We tend the inner child still aching and wounded. We see the long buried gift and affirm its beauty for the world. Our compassion tends the cry within until the suffering inside of us feels fully seen, heard, held, and healed.

As the suffering beneath my fury becomes ever more real for me, personified by this boy within me whose pain is still fresh, tender care rises up and flows through me. I want to assure the boy that he is alone no longer and wash away the lingering lies that he ever did anything to deserve being abandoned. I hold him. I let him weep. I let him know he will never be forgotten again. Not by me.

I sense my care flowing from a deeper source than inside myself. It shimmers with the cosmic compassion that saturates and sustains the vast totality of the universe. *Sensing the expansive sacredness*, I know in my bones that the heart of the universe breaks for this boy and holds him in an eternal care. This infinite expanse of compassion aches to seep into that boy and to bring him a healing certainty that he is forever held by love, forever seen and valued, even in a world where mothers are too wounded to remember their children alone in the dark. I invite this cosmic care to surround the suffering boy within me—as a healing light, an energy of love, a divine figure, or an iconic guardian from the past. It comes. And the boy knows he is held not only in my compassion but also in the compassionate face of the universe. He begins to heal, his primal terrors are soothed, and our connection with the sacred intensifies. In this space, we are one with the divine. We are lover and beloved, giver and receiver, all at once. We are held in the womb of infinite compassion. And infinite compassion holds and heals all wounds.

Such compassion restores our lives. New life is birthed and yearns to be fully embodied. We may find a trust in our worth, a confidence in our power, a sense of being beloved and beautiful, or a sense of awareness of the beloved beauty in others. *Embodying new life* recognizes the gifts and qualities budding within, and it longs to see them flourish. For me, I find that patience is growing within me, patience both for the bruises that continue to provoke my furies and for my loved ones who inadvertently brush up against my insecurities. In addition to this patience, I may feel a confidence in an enduring love that eases my dependency on others to assuage my sense of aloneness in the world. For the moment, my once erratic heart pulses with the heartbeat of compassion.

Paying attention, understanding empathically, loving with connection, sensing the sacredness, and embodying new life—this is the PULSE of compassion. This is the pulse of our hearts when restored to the natural essence of our core and caring Self. This is Self-compassion that flows from the essence of Self within us, and it extends to the suffering hidden within any interior movement whose cry wails from inside of us. Self-compassion heals, makes us whole, and connects us once more with the cosmic compassion whose face gazes from the depths of creation, weeping for our pain, and smiling at the beauty within us birthing into life.

CULTIVATING COMPASSION FOR YOURSELF

Welcoming Presence Meditation

1. Get grounded by taking several deep breaths and easing into an interior silence.

2. As your breathing continues, imagine and settle into an interior space that feels safe, grounding, peaceful, and receptive. It may help to imagine this as a specific place, either real or imaginary, that feels welcoming and sacred. For example, you can imagine a living room, a quiet chapel, a meadow, a beach, a warm cabin—any place that soothes you, centers you, and fills you with the promise of sacred presence.

3. As you relax into this interior space, intrusions may invade the quiet. These intrusions might be emotions, thoughts, inner voices, fantasies, body sensations, urges, or any other interior movement that ripples into your inner calm. Instead of shooing them away, being carried away by their power, or judging yourself for their presence within you, welcome them as guests within your interior space, your place of quiet. Here are some tips to assist you:

   › Refer to the intrusion in the third person. Instead of thinking *I am stressed right now*, think *Stress is present within me.*

> ❯ Express a welcoming attitude toward this intrusion. *I see you anxiety. Welcome. I allow you to be present within me.*

> ❯ Recognize the intrusion as a guest. *I trust you are here for a reason; you have some invitation for me. I may not know what it is, but I trust that you come with a gift.*

4. Ask the guest to express itself as an image—perhaps as an object like a coffeepot, chattering teeth, or a hive of buzzing bees; perhaps as a person or creature. Then, in whatever way feels right, honor and preserve this guest by placing it somewhere within your interior space. Perhaps you wrap it in a prayer shawl and place it on an altar. Maybe you place it in a gift box and put it on a shelf to open later. You might invite the guest to sit in a chair next to you. Or you can choose any other way of honoring its presence and allowing it to remain until a later time when you will become more fully acquainted.

5. Return to a sense of inner peace and gentle presence, reconnecting with your breath as needed to still and center you. Whenever you notice an interruption in this state of relaxed presence, welcome and receive that interruption as a guest in the same way that you welcomed and received other intrusions.

6. Invite a sacred presence you know—the Buddha, Allah, God, Jesus, the loving energy of the universe, a healing image, a beloved ancestor—to come and be with you and your guests in whatever way feels calming, healing, or restoring.

7. Before surfacing from this interior space, notice the gift you are receiving from the practice and allow that gift to flow throughout your entire body and extend into every part of your inner world.

8. In preparing to conclude this practice, discern if there is an invitation for how you might allow the gift of this practice to extend into your daily life.

(Note: This practice can be engaged through many different modes, of which interior meditation is but one. If you feel compelled, try this practice through other activities: writing, making a collage, drawing, working with clay, or playing music.

In the Moment

Over the course of your day, when you become aware of an interior movement threatening to possess you (a strong emotion, a powerful impulse to act in a certain way, a relentless inner voice, a bodily sensation, or a fantasy that has gripped you), ground yourself by taking some breaths. Notice the movement that is flooding you by saying to yourself, *I notice that* _____ *has come;* _____ *is present within me. I greet you* _____. Place the movement somewhere safe and contained within you.[8]

CULTIVATING COMPASSION FOR YOURSELF

Deepening Your Understanding of an Interior Movement

1. Recall one interior movement—a powerful emotion, a persistent inner voice, a compelling impulse to behave in some way—that has been a frequent companion in your life recently or one that you have found difficult to be with.

2. Take a few minutes and personify this interior movement, perhaps imagining it as a child or some creature that embodies the feelings of this movement. You can do this in your imagination, draw it, or find a picture on the Internet.

3. Spend some time *paying attention* to this personified emotion. Extend it a nonjudgmental and open presence of care that genuinely seeks to understand its experience. (Note: If you are not feeling open, nonjudgmental, and curious toward the child or creature and the interior movement it embodies, then another interior movement has slipped in—so notice that movement then invite it to relax until you genuinely feel open and curious toward the personified emotion.) Invite the interior movement to embody its experience by asking, *What gender would it be? How old would that creature be? What would it look like as it experiences this*

emotion (its facial expression, its bodily posture, its attire, and so forth)? What is this creature feeling and experiencing within the situation that activates it?

4. Just as you might with a child experiencing this interior movement, cultivate an *understanding* of the cry within the personified movement. Invite it to surface the deeper suffering underneath it through whichever of the FLAG questions reveals its pain:

> ❯ What is your deepest *fear* underneath the movement?

> ❯ What is your deepest *longing* underlying it?

> ❯ What *aching wound* do you carry that remains sensitive?

> ❯ What *gift* that you are trying to give me feels stifled or discouraged?

5. After you have finished this interview, invite the personified interior movement to summarize what it has shared with you through filling in the following:

   Whenever I (the personified interior movement) get activated during the day, I need you to hear and understand _____. In short, I long for _____.

6. After you have finished this interview, think of a physical object that represents or symbolizes this persistent interior movement. Make sure the object is something you can carry with you for a few days (for example a coin, stone, button, bead, cross, acorn, ring, paper clip, or eraser).

7. If it feels right to you, conclude your reflection by inviting any sacred reality you know—the Buddha, Allah, God, Jesus, the loving energy of the universe, a healing image, a beloved ancestor—to be with the personified interior movement in whatever way feels healing and life-giving.

IN THE MOMENT

Over the course of a few days, carry the symbolic object of the interior movement with you. At various times during the day, simply notice this object as a way of recognizing that this interior movement is a part of you that needs attention and care. Whenever you feel this interior movement becoming activated, tend to it with some variation of the following: Take a moment to breathe and ground yourself. Reconnect with the symbolic object that you are carrying. Notice that the interior movement is once more present by saying to yourself, *(The name of the interior movement) is here. I see you.* Ask the movement, *What do you need me to understand right now?* Assure the movement that you understand and will tend to its need. Invite the movement to relax and step to the side for now—perhaps returning into the object that carries it—until you are able to return to it and tend it more fully.

Chapter 4

Taking the Other's PULSE

Cultivating Compassion for Another

A friend of mine who works as a dance therapist attended a wedding reception. A small band played before a modest dance floor, and people clustered around the sea of round tables that spread throughout the reception hall. Sitting at one of the tables, she paused from the conversation and noticed an elderly gentleman in a wheelchair. He was threading his way through the tightly packed tables toward the nearly empty dance floor. Once he arrived there, he simply leaned back in his wheelchair and swayed back and forth to the music.

Something about the man moved her. My friend stood up, made her way to the dance floor, bent before the gentleman, and said, "Excuse me, sir. We don't know each other, but could I share this dance with you?"

With a wave of delight coming across his face, he said, "Why certainly, miss. It would be my pleasure."

For the next several minutes, the two of them danced. With grace and elegance, they glided up, down, and across the floor. Other couples moved to the side, those at the tables hushed and looked on, as these two twirled, rocked, and swayed as one to the rhythms of the music.

When the song ended, the audience applauded. The band members bowed in tribute, as well. The gentleman, still bright in the glow of the dance, looked at his partner and said, "Thank you, oh, thank you. It's been twenty years since I've danced. I used to be a dancer, you know. My how I have missed it. When I dance, I feel loved. When I dance, I feel the power of God lifting me up into life."

———————

Our acts of compassion restore both others and ourselves. They reconcile us to the love that soothes the soul and sustains the spirit. They move us to healing rhythms. With a sacred power, they lift us up into life. My friend's act, though spontaneous, embodied the PULSE of compassion. *Paying attention,* she noticed another human being—in this case, an elderly man in a wheelchair determined to get to a dance floor. *Understanding empathically,* she was moved by his yearning to move with the music, even if alone and of limited mobility. *Loving with connection,* a swell of care and generous regard filled her and flowed toward this man swaying by himself to the music. *Sensing the sacredness,* her care became a channel of a loving energy that hushed a room and lifted them all into life. *Embodying new life,* she yearned for and then celebrated the glowing vitality of a man who danced once more and felt himself beloved. To be sure, my friend's gesture of dancing with this stranger moved to the pulse of compassion.

The Precondition for Cultivating Compassion

My friend's compassion was rather instinctive. Such compassion for another can also be cultivated. The essential precondition, however, is that we are open to a compassionate encounter. When we are not open to a compassionate connection with someone—when we are feeling reactive, dismissive, frightened, overwhelmed, or even simply numb and distracted—an interior movement holds us in its grasp. Compelling a feeling of compassion at such times can seem fake and comes off instead as feigned civility or charity laced with our own agenda. In addition, it dismisses the cry of our interior movement and thus ignores the need or suffering hidden within it. This is internally contradictory. Coaxing a soft heart for another while hardening our hearts toward ourselves is, as previously mentioned, like straining to force relaxation. Something within us resists and digs in. This resistance is the unmet need or unhealed wound that continues to cry out from within us. When ignored, its suffering only intensifies, and it screams for attention in other ways—as compassion fatigue, a seething resentment, or a stomach churned to chronic upset. For the well-being of both body and soul, these interior cries must be recognized and heard.

This may be what most distinguishes the Compassion Practice from other methods of cultivating compassion. When encountering another, if we do not feel open to connection, we must first turn inward and tend the erratic pulse within us. Metaphorically, it is caring for the logs in our own eyes before focusing on the speck in the eye of another. This in no way is meant to demonize the movements within us that resist compassion. On the contrary, these movements guide us on the path through which we are restored to our Self. They signal the needs and wounds within us that require care before we can relax into our core and compassionate Self.

The key diagnostic tool to assess our readiness to cultivate compassion toward another is to ask ourselves, *Do I genuinely feel open to a compassionate connection with this person?* If we do not, we take the U-turn and notice the stirrings that have been activated within us. Like a skilled chiropractor assessing mobility and noting pain, we surface our antipathies and address the cries hidden within them. My vindictiveness toward another, for example, may be a plea for safety and protection. My numbness may be fatigue aching for renewal. My fierce busyness may be the panicked fight to keep from losing myself in chronic and ceaseless caretaking. In turning inward and taking the pulse of our activated states, a Self-compassion emerges that not only relaxes and satisfies our agitated movements, it forms the ground on which genuine compassion for another can be cultivated. We discover once more the capacities within us to truly love our neighbors with the very same love with which we love ourselves.

Once we are restored to a grounded Self-compassion, we return our attention toward the other person. Sometimes this is enough. Soothing the cries within our reactions may suffice to soften us into a place of care and understanding. Having tended the logs in our own eyes, we are able to see clearly again. Then, like my dance therapist friend, we may simply take notice of someone before us and feel an organic wave of affection filling and flowing through us.

Sometimes, however, more effort is required. We gaze at someone else and cannot help but see that a speck really is lodged within his or her eye. We are open to the person, but we are not necessarily moved by the person's presence or behavior. Cultivating a genuine compassion toward that person is still possible, and the process by which it is cultivated is informed by three core insights.

Other People Are Beloved by the Universe

First, the Compassion Practice recognizes that every being we encounter is inherently beloved. As observed in the Sermon on the Mount, the sun shines on the just and the unjust; the rain falls on the good and the evil. (See Matthew 5:43-48.) In like manner, the sacred energy of compassion that flows from the core of the universe extends to every being in creation. No matter how broken, marred, tortured, or twisted people might become, their wounds are grieved; their joys are celebrated; they are held securely in the cosmic compassion that sustains and restores all life.

Spiritual traditions attest to the belovedness of all. The essence of whatever we deem transcendent or sacred—Brahman, Nirvana, God, the Tao, the Force Field of Life, the Inhabitants of the Spirit World—is fundamentally compassion. And like the web of interconnectedness that Buddhists recognize, the circle of ancestors that indigenous traditions revere, or the face of God that Abrahamic faiths see in all aspects of creation, that sacred essence of compassion extends to every living creature. Each person we meet in the course of our days, in the course of our journeys—the person beside us when we wake in the morning, the attendant serving us coffee, the officer directing traffic, the motorist sitting in traffic—each one is held in the web of love. Each person is surrounded by a cosmic circle of care and beheld by a face whose eyes gaze upon him or her as beloved. Holding others in the light of this love opens our heart more fully toward them. And it deepens our connection to the cosmic compassion whose expansive reach extends even to those lost and in the margins of society.

A chaplain I know was visiting a hospital when he overheard two nurses talking. One was sharing that the police had shot a gang member who had executed a teenage girl. The gang member's death was imminent, but his heart was a match for a transplant uptown. The nurse listening was aghast. "Who," she asked with disgust, "would want the heart of such a monster?" According to the wisdom of the world's spiritual traditions, the cosmic heart of the universe would. And that heart would be broken, both for the young woman so brutally slain and for the horrors that gave rise to the tortured soul who would do it. When our own hearts can hold such compassion, we become instruments through which the sacred love of the universe holds and heals the world. In the face of our compassion, the person we behold catches a glimpse of the cosmic love of the universe.

Other People Bear the Pulse of Humanity

The second insight that grounds the cultivation of compassion toward others is that the pulse of humanity beats within the depths of anyone we encounter. In the same way that a caring core resides within each one of us, a fundamentally compassionate and intact Self dwells within every person we meet. Call it the Buddha nature of love and compassion, the divinely bestowed image of God, the ever-present Beloved Lover, or simply the steady ember of our truest Self, a compassionate connection resides within every human heart—no matter how damaged or hardened that heart may become.

It beats even in a heart as damaged as Damian's.

Damian was an eighth-grader at an inner city school in Toronto. With multiple tattoos and piercings, Damian looked as tough as he behaved. He challenged his teacher and was incapable of focusing on the work of the moment. He could not restrain his vocal impulses, and he was constantly on the edge of an angry outburst, even to the point of accosting other students if they got anywhere near him. The roots of his behavior were known. At four years old, Damian watched his father shoot and kill his mother. With his father in prison, his mother dead, and no other family to take him in, Damian spent the next ten years tossed among over twenty foster homes and several government facilities. Over time, his rage and aggression became increasingly impossible for him to contain. Now an eighth-grader, he was one assault away from a permanent stay in reform school.

To his teacher's trepidation, Damian was present when Mary Gordon visited the classroom. Gordon, founder of Roots of Empathy, had a unique method for cultivating empathic connection. She brought an infant, along with the baby's parents, to class for the students to observe. Damian resented the intrusion. Scowling with annoyance, he studied the situation from a perch across the room. The other students spent the morning cooing with the baby on a blanket and taking turns holding her. After some time, the mother announced that the baby needed to nap. To everyone's shock, Damian came over and asked if he could walk the baby to sleep. The teacher tried to caution the mother, but the mother felt an intuitive trust.

Damian slipped into a Snugli and carefully strapped the eight-month-old child in place against his chest. An instinctive care kicked in. Like a seasoned and affectionate father, Damian pressed her close and softly rocked her in his arms while gingerly walking around the room. The baby glanced for her mother at first, but then sensed that she was safe. Drowsy, she closed her eyes and after a while fell asleep. Damian grew wide-eyed with wonder. Careful not to wake her up but unable to contain his triumph, he nodded his enthusiasm to the others in the room and whispered to each one around, "Look, I got her to sleep. See, she's really sleeping."

Damian savored the moment, walking the room, cradling the child, and beaming for all who would see. When it was finally time for her to leave, Damian handed the baby to her mother. He caressed her head. He said good-bye. Then he turned to his teacher and asked, "Do you think if nobody ever loved you it's still possible to be a good dad?"

———

Though Damian has been damaged by horror and hardened by heartache, he still carries an unmarred face of compassion. His true Self contains an enduring capacity for care and connection. It is buried beneath the façade of hostility and hidden behind the scowls of rage, but it remains intact, lying in wait for the empathic connection that will coax it into the world. No matter how calcified our exterior shells may become, assaulted by the cruelties of life, the pulse of humanity beats within us. It is as instinctive as a tattooed truant rocking a baby to sleep in a Snugli.

In a world where heartache gives rise to all manner of aggression, we find it easy to demonize persons who disturb or offend us. We reduce them to the behaviors and distortions we find problematic. "My ex-wife is just vindictive and angry," we say to anyone who will listen. "That person with the abhorrent politics is an uncompromising, dogmatic bigot." "The eighth-grader who terrorizes the classroom is nothing but a cold-blooded thug." In demonizing others, we distance ourselves from their humanity. We forget that their hearts beat with longing and pain. For all practical purposes, we assume that the pulses of their spirits have been extinguished.

Damian reminds us otherwise. Every human being we encounter, even those we are tempted to write off and dehumanize, possesses the capacity for care and connection. An essence of Self resides deeply within them. They too hide an unmarred face of compassion that longs for connection.

Other People's Behaviors as FLAGs

The third insight that facilitates cultivating genuine compassion for others is the recognition that others' interior worlds are constructed in precisely the same way as our own. Every interior movement we encounter in others— their emotional reactions, their conversations and self-talk, their behaviors whether impulsive or deliberate—is a cry rooted in some form of suffering aching to be soothed, some need fighting to be secured, or some form of joy longing to be celebrated. Their emotions, words, and actions are FLAGs frantically waving for attention and care. Their actions rise out of life-threat-ening *fears*, unsatisfied *longings*, *aching wounds* still bleeding and raw, and *gifts* and capacities that are obstructed and stifled. Their actions may seem to be saying *I hate the world and everyone in it.* But underneath the vehemence lies a deeper cry: *I feel beaten down and alone. Someone please see me.*

The coworker who chastises us for failing to follow procedures may long simply to be taken seriously after a lifetime of feeling dismissed and deval-ued. The loved one who withdraws behind a mask of invulnerability may be terrified of rejection, aching to feel safe and understood. The eighth-grader who rages at anyone around may feel powerless and alone in a world where loved ones are slain right before his eyes.

Agitated emotions, cutting discourse, difficult behaviors, even acts of violence and violation are but the tragically veiled screams of people in pain aching to be heard, held, and healed. As counterproductive as it seems, destructive behavior and extreme emotions are desperate pleas for life and connection. They bid for power, significance, safety, and affiliation; they are rooted in wounds of abandonment, oppression, helplessness, and abuse.

To be sure, sometimes these words and deeds cause destruction. Damian's cry took the form of rage and aggression. The plea of a gang member dying on a gurney took the form of murder. The path of compassion in no way condones violation or minimizes the suffering violation can cause. It does, however, offer a basis for understanding that tempers the impulse to demonize and ostracize an offender. No one is born a perpetrator. Every act of violation is born from suffering and is a plea, sometimes grotesquely disguised, for healing and restoration. This insight opens a door to empathic connection. And, as Damian so powerfully demonstrated, empathic connection has the potential to soften a hardened heart and restore our capacities for caring reconnection.

Cultivating the PULSE of Compassion toward Others

Grounded in these insights, the Compassion Practice offers a way to cultivate a genuine compassion for others. It is important to remember that we only cultivate such compassion when we feel open to connecting with the other person. If we encounter someone and feel anything but compassion for him or her, we ground ourselves, take a U-turn, and tend to the stirrings within us until our erratic pulse is steady once more. When I react with fury at my son's tardiness in picking me up, I do not force a compassionate understanding toward him and his behavior. Instead, I turn inward, recognize my own hidden insecurities, and, through the PULSE of Self-compassion, settle once more in my caring and connected core. Only then, do I turn my attention back toward the person before me.

As I consider Justin and his tardiness, I come face-to-face with the speck that is still lodged within his eye—he remains late and his behavior does not inspire in me a spontaneous affection for him. How do I cultivate a compassionate connection with my son when it is not immediately forthcoming? I do so in precisely the same way I cultivated compassion for myself. I connect with the PULSE of his humanity—the bid for life that beats within him and the suffering he experiences when that life is obstructed. This pulse beats, however dimly or buried, beneath the surface of any presenting emotion or behavior. Connecting with it compassionately can be done as follows.

First, we *pay attention*. We simply notice nonreactively and nonjudgmentally what others are doing and what they look like while they are doing it. We gaze upon them contemplatively the way an artist would observe them or as if they were a character on stage or in a film. In the same way we cultivate a radical acceptance of every interior movement within us, we nurture a welcoming posture and expansive hospitality toward the people we are beholding. We trust that everything they do or feel has a reason and makes sense given the past they have known. With an open, nonreactive curiosity, we take a long, loving look at the reality of their experiences. We notice *their behaviors* (What are they actually doing, and what do they look like as they are doing it?), *their emotions* (What feelings are they experiencing, and how intensely are they feeling them?), *their words* (What are they saying, either internally or out loud, to us, to others, and to themselves?), and *their bodily expressions* (What do their bodies look like? What are the expressions on their faces? What are their postures and gestures? Do we notice any symptoms of stress or pain?) In short, we attempt to see them in the truth of their experiences.

As I attempt to see Justin in the truth of his experience, I might notice that he pulls up at ten after six with a lovely smile on his face as if savoring something truly delicious. Or he might exhibit a look of dread at how late he is or an unhurried oblivion to the time at all. If I find myself reacting, I take a momentary U-turn, reassuring the log that is edging back into my eye that its needs are heard and will be tended. Then I return my gaze to Justin and simply behold how he is present in this moment.

After taking the time to see others in the truth of their experience, we try to *understand empathically* the suffering underneath their actions or emotions. Their behavior, however distorted, is a bid for life or connection. Their emotions and impulses are cries. Something on which their very life depends is threatened or at stake. Empathic understanding is cultivated through listening deeply to others' experiences until the sources of their behavior surfaces. We surface this source by asking ourselves, *What is the waving FLAG straining to be heard within the cry of what they are doing?*

Fear. What do they seem to most deeply fear? What is at stake causing them to feel or behave in this way?

Longing. For what do they most deeply long? What essential needs for the flourishing of their lives do they seem to be straining for?

Aching wound. What pains or oppression from their past can you imagine is raw and sensitive, perhaps triggered in this moment?

Gift obstructed. What strengths and capacities buried within them seem stifled and discouraged, pleading to be claimed and nurtured?

When we hear the sources of the cries within them, something shifts inside of us. We are moved. Our hearts open a bit wider. And compassion for them rises within us. What might surface as I listen deeply to the cry within Justin's behavior? Perhaps Justin is savoring the start of a secret courtship too new to share with his family. Maybe he's so terrified of my criticism that he's rushing to get me while fighting back the tears of shame stinging his eyes. Or maybe he's simply relishing his summer freedom while dreading the relentless approach of the impending school year's oppressive schedules.

Understanding the deeper cry of another's soul has the capacity to move us—no wonder Justin is a few minutes late; no wonder he has that look on his face—and it activates a *loving connection* that holds him with soothing care. Like the parent who lingers at a bedroom doorway to gaze upon a sleeping child, compassion is deepened as we pause to extend grace and understanding. May my boy's first taste of love be sweet. May his shame truly yield to the light of his beauty. May his capacity to enjoy the moment be a healing balm from the demands of young adulthood.

When love is revived and allowed to flow through us, we are plugged into a cosmic compassion. A sense of sacredness may emerge, a sacredness that longs to bathe this beloved in a love both infinite and enduring. We might invite this presence to surround this person—as a healing light, an energy of love, a divine figure, an iconic guardian from the past. *Sensing the sacredness* and extending it toward the person we are beholding transforms this practice into a form of prayer. Justin is held in the light of grace—a grace that holds us both.

The love of the universe, fused with our own, aches for healing and restoration. I hope that Justin will know the glory of being fully alive in all of his unique beauty and giftedness. As compassion deepens, so does our desire to see others *embodying new life*, and we commit our intention to nurture such life into being. What fullness is unfolding in Justin—the delights of love? The grace of knowing himself as beloved? The eyes to notice the beauty that is present and the freedom to linger in its light? Our pulses beat strongly when others' deepest desires become our own desires for them.

As it turns out, Justin shares with me later that he is in love. And his beloved starts work at six each evening. He drives her to work and drops her off to squeeze in every possible second of their limited time together. Then he rushes over to pick me up hoping not to be too late. Connecting with the pulse of life beating within his behavior has the capacity to free and deepen my compassion for him. Of course I want him to savor every minute with his new love. Taking my PULSE first connected me to my compassionate core. Taking Justin's PULSE connects us to each other. Then compassion may flow freely once more.

Loving Our Enemies

Accessing our compassion and generous goodwill for a nineteen-year-old savoring the sweetness of first love or an elderly dancer now bound in a wheelchair requires only minimal work for many of us. What about people who are far more difficult? How do we cultivate compassion for those who truly threaten or repulse us? Loving our enemies is the radical call and life-giving invitation of the Compassion Practice. It is possible to feel genuine compassion even for those who offend and infuriate us. This is the lodestar to which many of the world's spiritual traditions point—we can learn to love ourselves, our neighbors, and even our enemies.

In a world where violence, mean-spiritedness, aggression, and defiance ravage our cities and homelands, permeate our political discourse, and bleed into our schools, families, and places of work, offering compassion to our enemies may be the most pressing social challenge of our day. The future of our planet, communities, and interpersonal relationships depends on finding grounded, nonreactive, nonescalating ways of responding to others when we feel threatened or diminished. The future of our soul depends on it too. For learning to love our enemies is the spiritual path to our own healing, vitality, and personal transformation.

We find the clue for cultivating such radical compassion in what constitutes a person as our enemy. Our enemies are people who repel us. Literally. The word *enemy* comes from the Latin union of *in* (meaning "not") and *amicus* (meaning "friend" and linked to *amare* meaning "love"). Loved ones are people to whom we feel attracted and with whom we want to connect. Enemies are people we anti-love, so to speak. They are people from whom we recoil. Connection with them feels abhorrent. Like two positively charged magnets defying contact, we resist proximity to our enemies. Emotionally, we push them away, or we pull ourselves away in aversion. This repelling energy can take many forms—rage, disgust, contempt, terror, mockery, or apathy. For us, such people restrict our impulse of compassion.

We all have such people in our lives. Every day we encounter

People whose political or ideological views are repugnant to us—proponents of pro-choice, pro-life, immigration reform, or stronger borders;

People within certain social positions of which we are inherently suspicious—the poor, the wealthy, the military, the incarcerated;

People in the news or in our communities whose deeds particularly disgust us—acts of abuse, embezzlement, debauchery, infidelity;

People we encounter throughout the day who simply push our buttons—reckless drivers, inconsiderate neighbors, people who text while we are talking to them;

Even our friends, family, companions, and coworkers can be our "enemies" for a moment when they act in a way that triggers our fury or displeasure.

While we all have such enemies in our lives, it is revealing to recognize that we do not have the same ones. The telemarketer who incites my wrath prompts another's patient politeness, while the welfare recipient who infuriates that person stirs yet another's kind regard. In fact, the very same people that trigger us one day can evoke our understanding the next. While we are tempted to insist that another's offensive behavior is inherently repulsive and defies all capacity to be met with compassion, the truth is otherwise. Compassion toward this person is possible; yet, we obstruct it. The source of our repulsion lies within us. Something in us has conspired to knock us off the ground of our core and caring Self. The obstruction within us is some part of ourselves crying for care, and it is fighting to get our attention.

People who repel us are not arbitrary. They fit a profile that is unique to each of us. Only particular types of people ignite a heightened charge of reactivity within me—certain character traits, behaviors, or expressions on people's faces. For each of us, our enemies are custom-made. The reason for this is counterintuitive. People by whom we are repelled activate some part of ourselves that we have repressed—a part that we are refusing to look at, preoccupied, as we are, by the person who is repelling us. Our reactivity is the cry of something within us that is screaming to be noticed. When we ignore that cry—when we internally repel it—our repulsion toward the other intensifies.

In short, our enemies serve as mirrors. They reflect to us that which we have relegated to the shadows of our own inner world. Our resistance to holding them with compassion is rooted in a resistance to holding ourselves with compassion. That which we find untouchable in them is tethered to something we find untouchable within us. These parts within us, consigned to the shadows, are usually one of the following:

An unhealed wound. Parts of us still carry the pain of having been wounded in precisely the same way we see our enemies bringing pain to the world.

A secret shame. Parts of us are capable of precisely the same behaviors we reject in our enemies, and we fear that if these parts are revealed, we will be rendered equally untouchable.

A threatened life-need. Parts of us needing to flourish in life or love feel threatened or jeopardized—a need to feel safe, to be seen, to have value, or to feel included.

An undeveloped gift or power. Capacities within us (personal power; our voices, strengths, talents) have been chronically stifled by persons our enemies represent.

These buried parts of us long to see the light of day. Unhealed wounds ache to be acknowledged and held. Secret shames ache to know compassion and forgiveness. Essential life-needs ache to be satisfied. Stifled gifts ache to be claimed and to flourish. As long as we repel these parts of ourselves from within, they will seek alternative ways to get our attention. Our repulsion toward others is their scream for care. When others repel us, compassion invites us to refrain from attacking or villainizing our enemies or even shunning them in disgusted aversion. Instead, compassion invites us to turn inward—to hear the cry within us, tend its needs, heal its wounds, nurture its vitality. In so doing, we return to the Self-compassion that relaxes the reactivity within us and restores the pulse of our humanity. Over the course of the process, our enemies will be transformed. We will recognize them as human. They are people in pain just as we are. And the tether of our repulsion softens into the bond of compassionate connection.

An Enemy Transformed on the Softball Field

I love to play softball. I love to catch fly balls, swing the bat, and run the bases. I play the game just for the joy of it; in fact, I don't even like to keep score. I don't care who wins. I don't have a competitive bone in my body.

In other words, I am nothing like my teammate Matt.

Matt is a hothead. He slams into the catcher even if he can avoid it. He berates us—his teammates—when we make errors. He taunts opponents when they lose, and he argues with the umpires even if he's out by a mile. Quite frankly, I despise guys like Matt. He ruins the game. He's a bully. He's an embarrassment to our team. Of one thing I am certain: I could never be like him.

One day, an opposing team was one player short. I was afraid they would have to forfeit, and we would all have to go home. So I offered to play for the other team. After all, I didn't care who wins. Besides, I still got to play left field.

The game was an epic battle between two equally matched teams. We led by three runs; they caught up. They led by two runs; we caught up. Another rally, another lead change. Back and forth it went until we were ahead by two in the final inning. But Matt's team tied it up in the bottom half putting us into extra innings. We were all getting into it, even the crowd. Players from adjacent fields, their games long since over, stood around and cheered as the marathon game continued. We scored twice in the tenth, and Matt's team tied it up. Three more runs for us in the eleventh. Three more runs tie it up for Matt. Every lead was matched taking us to thirteen innings, fourteen innings, all the way to the fifteenth inning. We scored one more run, and then Matt's team came to bat. With one out, Matt was on third base, another runner was on second, and I was out in left field.

And I knew *exactly* how Matt was going to play this. Any ball hit to the outfield for the second out, he was going to tag up and bolt for home bowling through anybody in his path to score the tying run. *Well, not on my watch!*, I thought. For once, I was going to put this guy in his place. I positioned myself an extra step back so as to make a running catch with the momentum to throw Matt out at the plate. Sure enough, a soft line drive was hit to left field. I lined it up in my sight. Matt was prepped at third. The catcher was shaking at home. I could just see it all happening. I was going to make a running catch and throw the ball to home plate. And Matt would be out.

The ball came. I lunged to catch it. I took a step, grabbed the ball, and heaved it to home plate. But wait. Something was wrong. The ball was not in my mitt. It was not at my feet. It was not anywhere in front of me. I turned around and looked behind me. In my haste, I had run right past the ball. I watched it bounding out toward the parking lot beyond the field as Matt not only scored the tying run from third but the runner on second scored the winning run as well. And I—the meek and noncompetitive guy who does not care who wins—took my mitt, threw it to the ground, and verbally berated myself.

"How could you be so stupid?" I seethed. "In front of God and everybody, you made a complete ass of yourself!" I stomped and kicked with such agitation I could not settle down to walk through the congratulatory handshake line. I stormed to my car and fumed all the way home.

Once home, I realized that I had to teach a class on compassion first thing the following morning. Without a better idea, I decided to try the Compassion Practice. So I caught my breath and got grounded. I took the U-turn instead of seething at Matt. Shame burned within me. I could just see myself standing in left field, throwing a tantrum, and storming around. I watched that man. Then something happened. The man I saw started swelling up like a balloon. It was weird. It was like all the rage and venom within him was too much for his body to contain. So he began expanding—an overinflated doll with my likeness getting bigger and bigger, a balloon like those that fly in the Macy's Thanksgiving Day Parade. He kept expanding until finally he just exploded. Balloon fragments blew all over the field. And all that was left, like the man behind the curtain in *The Wizard of Oz*, was a runty, seven-year-old boy. It was me when I was a kid in Little League, relegated to right field because I was so bad, praying to God that nobody hit the ball to me because I couldn't stand the shame of dropping it again in front of everyone. And the little boy looked up at the adult me and simply said, "Why do you hate me so much?"

I realized he was right. I cannot stand people who belittle others for not being able to play well. I cannot stand them because I am just like them. I don't do it to others; I do it to myself. I hated the boy within me who had a hard time just catching the ball and ached for someone to understand his humiliation. Restored to my right mind, I could look at my younger self with compassion. I could let him know that I see him. And he no longer has to worry. In my eyes, he's a star—no matter how many balls he drops.

Then something else dawned on me too. Matt harbored a little boy as well. I turned my gaze toward him. My shame had long since dissipated. So had my disgust. I could see Matt more clearly, pumping his fist in exhilaration after the win. But his eyes betrayed something else. His aggression on the field was his cry. Would anyone see the right fielder in him and understand just how humiliated he feels?

———————

The people who repel us are our mirrors. They reflect to us the buried parts of ourselves that cry out for healing and wholeness. Matt surfaces in me a self-berating that taunts my own failure as severely as any bully on a ball field. And deeper still, I find a banished boy whose shame aches for care and compassion. These shadowed parts of me long for the light of day. So they project themselves onto people in my world who embody and rebound the repelling energy back at me. If I persist in ignoring these interior cries, they only scream louder. My repulsions toward others intensify. And sometimes these cries break through altogether in outbursts of rage and self-loathing that catch me off guard.

The secret to genuinely loving our enemies is to work with—not against—the momentum of our souls. Trying to compel a compassion for Matt when he personifies those qualities I despise in myself is like biking into a one hundred-mile-per-hour headwind that only gets stronger as I keep pedaling into it. Taking the U-turn, I can ride the tailwind that takes me back home to my Self. Once there, I find the wounded boy longing for arms that will receive him. From my compassionate core, I can welcome him and soothe his ancient terror. He is loved. And he needs nothing from any ball field to prove it. As I settle deeply into the pulse of my loving humanity, I might turn my gaze from the young boy to someone else. With eyes starving for love as well, the wounded boy in Matt stares at me. And in my compassionate core, he too is welcome.

In this way, our enemies are our spiritual teachers. They serve as allies on the road to life and love. They have the unique capacity to surface within us what most immediately longs for healing and wholeness. And in pointing us back to our Self, they lead us back to the source of compassion—a compassion wide enough to hold all the world's wounded. Our enemies can be our guides. They are the faces of grace in disguise.

CULTIVATING COMPASSION FOR ANOTHER

Hearing the Cry of a Beloved or Friendly Other

1. Choose a loved one, friend, or acquaintance for whom you have some affection to be the focus for this exercise. Imagine that person involved in a behavior or experiencing an impulse or emotion that feels difficult for him or her.

2. Take his or her PULSE and cultivate a deeper understanding of what he or she might be experiencing by answering the FLAG questions. It may be necessary to use your imagination and speculate at points.

   (Important note: If you find yourself reactive or activated in any way whatsoever, recognize your feelings and invite the activated emotion, judgment, or impulse within you to relax so you can observe and reflect on this person.)

   Paying attention. Describe nonjudgmentally what you see about this friend or loved one as you observe him or her experiencing the difficult feeling, impulse, or behavior.

   > What is his or her appearance—clothes, hair, expression?

   > What is his or her behavior?

> What does he or she seem to be feeling?

> What else might he or she be experiencing in this situation?

> What else might be going on in his or her life that contributes to what is happening?

Understanding empathically. Using your imagination if necessary, sense what may be the deeper suffering underneath his or her behavior using the FLAG technique.

> What might be his or her deepest *fears*?

> What might he or she most deeply be *longing* for?

> What persistent and *aching wounds* may he or she be carrying that could exacerbate the pain of the situation?

> What *gifts* might he or she possess that are being frustrated or denied at this time?

3. Summarize your sense of his or her experience by completing the sentences below. If his or her behavior were a cry of suffering, it would say the following:

> "Please understand . . . "

> "I ache for . . . "

> "Right now I most need . . . "

4. Write a prayer to a significant sacred presence in his or her life, a prayer that expresses what he or she would most deeply want the sacred to know about his or her pain, longings, or deepest needs. (If he or she is not religious, write it as a letter to someone, either living or dead, who provides a healing and sacred presence in his or her life.) Write the prayer or letter in the first person from his or her perspective.

CULTIVATING COMPASSION FOR ANOTHER

The Compassion Practice with a Difficult Other

1. ***Catch your breath.*** Ground yourself in a way that is most helpful to you: listen to music, read a sacred text, light a candle, or sit in silence. Take several deep breaths and ease into an interior space that feels safe, grounding, perhaps sacred.

2. *Take your PULSE.*

   Paying attention. Allow into your awareness various persons for whom you have difficulty feeling compassion—persons whose behavior or attitudes have triggered some form of reactivity within you recently. Of the various persons who have come to you, allow one to be the focus for this practice.

   For a moment, imagine that person and his or her behavior you find difficult. In your imagination, ask that person to recede into some sequestered room, away over the horizon, or into the light of the sacred so you can feel safe from his or her presence and influence.

   Turn your attention inward, and notice the feeling impulse or internal movement this person activated within you. Don't let it take you into its power, but don't judge or suppress it either. Simply cultivate a nonjudgmental awareness that this movement is present within you.

If you feel open to understanding this movement more deeply, proceed. If not, notice what you are feeling instead and invite that feeling to relax.

Understanding empathically. Invite this interior movement to surface the threatened need, sensitive wound, secret shame, or stifled gift underlying the movement's intensity. If it is helpful, invite it to express itself as a person (a child, an angel, an older adult) or an object (a hot iron, a hammer). Ask this interior part of you whichever FLAG questions allow a deeper understanding and compassion within you.

> What is your deepest *fear*?

> What is your deepest *longing*?

> What *aching wound* still bleeds within you?

> What hidden *gift* feels stifled and frustrated?

Loving with connection. Let yourself feel a sense of compassionate connection to whatever part of you surfaces from within. Care for this part of you just as you would love a wounded or frightened child.

Sensing the sacredness. Invite an expansive sense of sacredness—a healing light, a soothing breeze, the presence of a divine figure, a compassionate ancestor, a mentor—to be with this part of you in healing and life-giving ways.

Embodying new life. Notice any new life or perspective that is emerging within you and allow this gift to flow throughout your body and into every part of your being.

If it feels right to cultivate compassion toward the difficult other, invite this interior part of you to relax so you can simply gaze upon this difficult person. Invite this part of you to rest on the side, to safely inhabit your prayer space, or to remain in the presence of a sacred reality like a healing light or a divine figure. When you feel open to observing the difficult person, turn and focus your attention on him or her.

3. *Take the other's PULSE.*

> **Paying attention.** Remember this person at a time when he or she was involved in the behavior that feels offensive. For a few moments, observe what he or she is doing and the particular way he or she is doing it without judgment or reactivity. Watch with an open curiosity like an artist preparing to paint a subject.

> › What does the person look like—attire, facial expression, body posture?

> › How does the person behave? What does he or she say? What emotions does he or she feel?

> (Note: If you become activated, invite that reaction within you to relax—you are simply paying attention to this person.)

> **Understanding empathically.** Remember that what this person says or does is rooted in some suffering—his or her behavior is a cry aching to be heard and tended. Cultivate a deeper understanding of the suffering hidden underneath his or her behavior by engaging the FLAG questions:

> › What seems to be his or her deepest *fear*?

> › What is his or her deepest *longing*?

> › What *aching wound* seems to be stinging him or her right now?

> › What *gift* seems to be frustrated and is fighting to be recognized?

> **Loving with connection.** If it emerges, let yourself feel a sense of compassionate connection to the suffering underneath the person's behavior

just as you would love a wounded or frightened child who needs care. Extend that compassion toward the other person.

Sensing the sacredness. If it feels right, notice if an expansive sense of sacredness is near and invite that presence—as a healing light, a gentle breeze, a divine figure, an image or symbol—to be with this person at the source of his or her suffering, tending him or her in whatever way feels healing and restoring.

Embodying new life. Sense the new life that yearns to be birthed within him or her and extend your desire for this healing or life to flourish.

4. *Decide what to do.* Sense if there is an invitation for one concrete way to stay true to what you have experienced in the practice when you encounter this person again. This might mean discerning ways to claim what you need for life, power, dignity, and wholeness. Or it might mean discerning ways to embody compassion for the other by remembering an image of this person in his or her suffering, carrying a symbol of your intention to react from a caring space, or thinking of a word or phrase that helps you remember this person as a beloved and sacred human being.

In the Moment

Before you encounter this person again, take a few moments and imagine different actions, practices, or gestures that can help you stay grounded in your core when you are with him or her, especially when he or she behaves in ways that knock you off-center. Such actions might include the following:

> taking deep breaths

> visualizing your sacred space or a sacred image

> touching a symbol or object kept in your pocket

> glancing away and connecting with something in nature

> imagining light surrounding you and/or the other person

> ❯ touching your heart

> ❯ connecting with your body

> ❯ repeating a silent mantra to yourself such as *I am beloved*

> ❯ silently remembering the Serenity Prayer or the Jesus Prayer

> ❯ squeezing your index finger

> ❯ curling your toes

Experiment with these grounding actions for a few weeks. Whenever you are with this difficult person (or any other difficult person), practice actions like the ones above and notice what helps you stay grounded during such encounters. If it feels right, you may try to listen for the cry that is hidden underneath the person's words and behavior. Try to remember his or her suffering and humanity. See what it is like to remain grounded and connected to another's humanity.

Chapter 5

Deciding What to Do

Discerning Compassionate Action

On a Friday morning in November of 2013, villainy descended upon San Francisco. A damsel in distress was tied to a bomb on the tracks of an approaching cable car. The evil mastermind who plotted the diversion was robbing a bank downtown. Lou Seal, the beloved Giants baseball mascot, was kidnapped and caged at AT&T Park. The city, held hostage to rampage and terror, was in dire need of a hero.

One came from a most unlikely place.

Five-year-old Miles Scott lives in Tulelake, California—a small farm town near the Oregon border and hundreds of miles from any metropolis. Miles was too young to know much about villainy. Or at least he should have been. As an infant, Miles suffered from constant fatigue, spikes of fever, chronic bone pain, bruising, and absence of appetite. At eighteen months, doctors diagnosed him with acute lymphoblastic leukemia, a rare form of blood cancer that could be fatal within weeks if left untreated.

For the next few years, Miles's childhood was all but stolen. While other children battled phantom foes and rival siblings, Miles fought cancer. With his father, a hay farmer, and his mother, a young farmwife, holding vigil beside him, he occupied hospital beds far from home in the distant cities of Medford and Portland. His early years were consumed by long stays in intensive care, course after course of radiation treatments, perpetual bouts with nausea and fatigue, an endless stream of needles, lab tests, toxic drugs, blood cell counts, and long stretches where the only food he could absorb came through an IV in his arm.

Miles did, however, have a healing refuge. He loved to watch *Batman* on TV with his dad. For hours on end, with Miles too weak to lift his head off the pillow, the two of them escaped into Gotham City through reruns of the original Adam West series. Miles so took to Batman that a cape became his standard attire. In the hospital, at cancer treatment facilities, and during his brief respites at home, Miles dressed up as the Caped Crusader. No villain was too evil for him to take down; as Batman, death itself could be faced and defied. The superhero was so at one with Miles's identity that when asked his deepest wish, he said he wanted to be Batman for real, for a day.

So the Make-A-Wish Foundation decided to make it happen. The organization, dedicated to sustaining the spirits of children fighting life-threatening illness, made a deal with Miles. Through the dark days of chemotherapy and radiation and the endless nights of their gruesome side effects, Miles would hold onto his dream like a lifeline. And when his treatment was completed, he would get his wish. He would go to San Francisco, stay in a high-rise hotel, and be Batman for real, for a day.

Miles had no idea what awaited him.

By the time Miles and his family trekked to the city, they were primed for a celebration. Only a couple of months after his final treatment, the chemo port in his chest now removed, the five-year-old Miles was officially in remission. After taking on leukemia and winning, he was ready for other less ravaging opponents. As far as he knew, however, he was only coming to the city to get properly outfitted. All that he was told at the outset of the trip was that the Make-A-Wish Foundation wanted to present him with his very own custom-made Batkid suit. No Halloween costume and cape anymore; Miles would have a suit so real and life-like that he would refuse to take if off—even at bedtime. He received it Thursday evening. It fit him and his bed perfectly.

Friday morning, as directed, Miles's dad turned on the TV. The local news, an accomplice to Make-A-Wish's scheme, declared a citywide alert. Mayhem was brewing in Gotham. Commissioner Gordon—the real-life Chief of Police, Greg Suhr—came onto the screen with an emergency plea: "Batman, we need you . . . and please bring Batkid."

Miles's dad turned to him in amazement and said, "Miles, that's you!"

They rushed to the hotel lobby, Miles already fully attired. A black Lamborghini, decaled and accessorized as an authentic Batmobile, pulled up. Batman, decked out in an adult-sized version of the same suit Miles was wearing, leaped out and said, "Batkid, they need us." Miles hopped in. Flanked by a police escort worthy of a dignitary—lights flashing, motorcycles in formation—they made for Nob Hill. Reports had come in—a damsel was in distress.

Sure enough, a woman was tied to a bomb on railroad tracks with a clanging cable car on the horizon. Hundreds of onlookers flocking the streets were chanting, "Batkid, Batkid." Miles got out of the car and looked around, a bit overwhelmed. But Batman reminded him a woman was in peril; she needed Batkid. The pint-sized superhero rose to the challenge. He clenched his fists, tightened his lips, and rushed toward the danger with great determination. He pulled the wires to deactivate the bomb and untied the terrified woman. The crowd cheered, the cable car stopped, and the woman knelt down and embraced her rescuer. Batkid had saved her. Miles patted her shoulder, still taken aback by all that he had just witnessed.

Unfortunately, there was no time to rest. The Riddler had been spotted sneaking into a bank in the financial district. Jumping back into the Batmobile, the Dynamic Duo raced downtown. Another chanting crowd awaited with posters boasting *Batkid Rocks* and *I Believe in Batkid*. As they pulled up, Batkid rushed into the bank, spied the culprit, and trapped the Riddler inside a locked vault. The police came, cuffed the bandit, and emerged from the bank with the victorious hero to display the villain now in custody. The crowd cheered—and it was growing. Even passersby were stopping to see what was happening.

Buoyed by the joyous commotion, the heroes took a break for burgers and milkshakes in Union Square. The crowd followed like fans would celebrities. A crowd numbering in the thousands filled the plaza; people climbed trees and shimmied up lampposts to catch a glimpse of Batkid in the café. Impromptu signs pervaded the throng—*Batkid Is Our Hope*, *You're Our Hero*, and *SF Loves Batkid*. In front of the restaurant, a flash mob erupted dancing to the Journey song "Don't Stop Believin'." The entire crowd sang along. A spontaneous festival erupted right in the heart of the city.

But wait. The Penguin had kidnapped the Giants mascot. As one, the crowd chanted, "We need Batkid. We need Batkid." Batkid, growing more confident in his powers by the minute, flashed a thumbs-up from the restaurant window. He was on it. Back at the Batmobile, Miles and Batman raced to AT&T Park where they frantically searched for the captive mascot. Batkid freed Lou Seal from a cage and spotted the Penguin trying to escape. A wild chase ensued throughout the ballpark until Batkid tackled the Penguin on the field. The media took pictures. Batkid saved the day once more, and the city decided to show its gratitude.

In front of the ballpark, a police motorcade arrived with sirens and fanfare worthy of a World Series championship parade. Navigating through cheering crowds now six deep on the sidewalk, the Batmobile headed toward City Hall. A crowd of some twenty thousand people had gathered—many of them recruited volunteers, many more onlookers caught up in the excitement. The San Francisco mayor, a US Justice department attorney, the Chief of Police, the editor of the city paper, and the Regional Director of the FBI were waiting for Batkid to arrive. The mayor gave Batkid a key to the city and deputized him as a federal agent. The *San Francisco Chronicle* unveiled a special edition of the next day's paper with the headline "Batkid Saves City." And in response to the raucous cheers, Miles raised his arms in triumph and unmasked himself for all to see. Miles from Tulelake was Batkid. Miles from Tulelake was the fearless victor over villainous foes.

People from across the world were moved by Miles's story. Facebook posts and Twitter images from Italy, the United Kingdom, Australia, and Korea celebrated Batkid. Even Washington, D.C. appreciated the depths of Batkid's heroism. President Obama sent a video from the White House in which he summed up the sentiments of those around the world. "Way to go, Miles!" he declared from the Oval Office. "Way to save Gotham."

Yes. Way to go, Miles. And while we are at it, way to go, Gotham. Way to replenish the spirit in a child. Way to replenish ours as well.

The Restorative Power of Compassionate Action

For a five-year-old boy battling leukemia, San Francisco is a city, as the Chief of Police later observed, "with its heart in the right place." It is a heart that beats to the pulse of compassion. The people were touched by the tenacity of a child with cancer who fought and defeated the illness that would take him. They understood his longing for superhero powers to take on the forces that threaten life. And they were poised to celebrate those powers being claimed—in Miles's pint-sized earnestness, his revelry in the fantasy, his fist pumps of victory, and the joy of his childhood dream fulfilled.

This abundance of compassion went far beyond sentiment. It began there—with people moved by a boy's pain and longing—but it did not end there. It incarnated such sentiment into concrete acts of kindness, care, encouragement, and restoration. These acts proliferated throughout the city—designers crafted costumes, car dealers loaned Lamborghinis, inventors constructed elaborate props, flash mob organizers choreographed dance moves, newspapers printed special editions, public officials made media appearances, thousands drove in from around the city to decorate placards and populate the chanting crowds. Compassion begs for embodiment. Without action, compassion becomes sentimentality. Embodied compassion can touch the soul of another and galvanize a city along the way.

As exemplified in San Francisco, acts of compassion restore us. To be sure, they buoy the spirits of those who are suffering. Caring presence beside the bedridden, casseroles left on a doorstep, notes of encouragement found in the mailbox, a wordless embrace when a loved one has passed—acts of care and kindness can stoke the embers of the human spirit when affliction threatens to dim them. Embodied compassion on Batkid Day helped a five-year-old cancer survivor come to discover the superhero powers already within him. He is the boy, after all, who can take on the forces that threaten life. His outstretched arms and beaming smile on a dais in front of City Hall were evidence enough. Through a city's extravagant kindness, Miles Scott's wish had come true—he was Batman for real and for more than a day.

Acts of compassion also restore the people moved to embody them. Extending kindness feels good. Taking some time to care for another replenishes the pulse of our spirits as well. It frees us from the impulses that deaden and disconnect us. It grounds us once more in who we really are—the core Self that composes our truest essence. And it deepens our connection to the boundless spirit of goodwill that gives us life and sustains our hope. The satisfaction on the faces of the innumerable volunteers testifies to this restorative power of compassion. Many of them ditched work or school to take part. To them, it was more than worth it. Their hearts, opened to Miles's plight, expanded even further in acting on their compassion. One volunteer, having driven a hundred miles merely to be an extra in the crowd celebrating Batkid, summed it up this way: "Imagining that child in intensive care, then seeing him glow with his hands in the air, I have to be honest. I felt selfish. I'm the one leaving with hope for the future." Love resuscitates life within us.

Acts of kindness also restore those looking from the sidelines. Compassion is contagious. Seeing a person care for another can inspire care within us as well. In San Francisco, pedestrians, tourists, cab drivers, cyclists, even bankers and lawyers extending their lunch breaks, were captured by the fervor of compassion. The multitudes at City Hall—along with those around the world watching through Facebook posts, Twitter, and cell phone videos—found genuine inspiration in the heroism of a five-year-old cancer survivor and in the heroics of kindness that shouldered and celebrated him. What began as the wish of a boy fighting cancer in a rural town in California became a worldwide outpouring of kindness. This expanding circle of care renewed the spirits of all drawn into its reach. It offered a glimpse of the transcendent force that truly can transform the evils of our planet—the contagion of compassion that has the power to unite the human community.

The Dark Knight, the guardian of good in the world, would be proud.

Embodied Compassion in the World

Spiritual traditions affirm that genuine compassion is embodied in acts of restorative care, and they offer insights on the forms that embodied compassion can take. Jewish teachings invite the faithful into the practice of *tikkun olam*—"repairing the world." Those who live true to the God of compassion and liberation devote themselves to acts of healing, hospitality, kindness, and justice. Care is especially extended to the vulnerable and to those in need—the widows, orphans, outcasts, and strangers. In some Kabbalistic traditions, each concrete act of compassion is a miracle unto itself—a miracle of kindness that consecrates the world and weds it more fully, one fragment at a time, with the Holy One who created it.[1]

Christian teachings likewise promote acts of compassion. Being the body of Christ in the world means feeding the hungry, clothing the naked, visiting the imprisoned, and freeing the oppressed. Jesus was not only a mystic and spiritual teacher but also a peacemaker and prophet of social transformation. He instructed his followers to cultivate the *kin-dom* of God on earth.[2] This kin-dom, like Martin Luther King's vision of the Beloved Community, promotes justice, mutuality, sanctuary, and inclusivity. Jesus modeled it through his radical practice of table fellowship. In a culture where only those deemed ceremoniously "clean" were allowed to dine at a ritually pure household, Jesus invited all to his table—the sick and the lame, lepers and prostitutes, tax collectors, traitors. the poor, and centurions. The kin-dom of God is a social order that reflects God's loving essence. As such, it embodies what Marcus J. Borg calls the "politics of compassion."[3]

Buddhism also affirms that the impulse of compassion pulsates into the embodiment of concrete action. Meditation and mindfulness lead to a deepened awareness of both the suffering of others and our interdependence with them. Through threads that weave everyone in the world into a single web, each person contributes to the suffering of another, and each person participates in the other's liberation. Enlightenment is not complete until all are freed from the snares of suffering and deception. In recent years, "Socially Engaged Buddhism," led by the likes of Thich Nhat Hanh and the Dalai Lama, highlights the political implications of Buddhist spiritual practice.[4] Compassion not only eases others' suffering but also works to transform the social conditions that support and perpetuate their suffering. Compassion works for justice; yet it does so compassionately. It preserves the dignity of all human beings and transforms the violent passions in us. It recognizes our interconnection even with those who are brutal and abusive, and it extends the invitation of restored relationship to anyone willing to receive it.

True compassion is engaged. It expresses itself in tangible ways. The forms of such engagement are varied. Compassionate action can be embodied as the following:

Generosity. Compassion often takes the form of offering resources to ease others' suffering. Giving money to a tsunami relief organization or to a homeless person on a curb can flow from our genuine care and concern. Donations to the Make-A-Wish Foundation skyrocketed in the wake of Batkid's sojourn through San Francisco.

Service. Perhaps most commonly, compassion takes the form of caring directly for the immediate needs of those who are suffering—nursing the sick, feeding the hungry, sitting with the griefstricken, clearing rubble after a disaster, helping the injured find medical assistance. Acts of healing, care, kindness, and presence offer material comfort and spiritual balm. Thousands of such acts—some rather simple, others quite elaborate—tended the needs and buoyed the spirits of Miles Scott and his family.

Witness. Compassion can involve bearing witness of the plight of those who suffer—vigils for peace and freedom abroad, prayer services for children abused, street corner signs in protest of the dumping of chemical waste, bumper stickers pleading to end human trafficking. In Buenos Aires, the *Madres de Plaza de Mayo*, known also as the "Mothers of the Disappeared," gathered weekly for decades in peaceful opposition to the thousands of children abducted, tortured, and buried in unmarked pits. Their presence not only solidified resistance to a brutal military regime but also emboldened other woman around the globe to stage similar protests for indignities in their homelands.

Solidarity. Compassion can take the radical form of sharing the plight of those whose suffering eludes short-term remedies—living on skid row; working alongside day laborers; moving to Zimbabwe, Haiti, or South Central Los Angeles; serving the destitute in Gaza or Calcutta. Such acts of solidarity are profound subversions of the social orders that keep us separate.

Empowerment. Compassion can go beyond attending to the material needs of those who suffer. Compassion can empower them with the skills, tools, and personal capacities to sustain their own survival and flourishing. Acts of empowerment recognize the subtle dependency that long-term caregivers can inadvertently encourage, and it evades the threat of paternalism that can creep unconsciously into service providers. Empowerment is the difference between bringing fish to the hungry and teaching them how to fish. It is the difference between being the superhero that saves a child's life and helping the child discover the superhero already within him. Both have their places. Both serve life. Care without empowerment breeds dependency; empowerment without care subverts the spirit.

Justice. Finally, compassion can attend to the structural causes that give rise to suffering in the first place. The pain that moves us is nestled within social conditions that perpetuate it. People ravaged by hunger, discrimination, violence, and disease live within a web of social complexities. Their affliction is rooted in and aggravated by power inequities, cultural prejudices, unjust economic systems, inattentive institutional policies, and oppressive political powers. And suffering will continue as long as the social structures that sustain it remain unchecked and untransformed. Compassionate action, therefore, can take the form of public advocacy, political lobbying, education, reform campaigns, non-violent resistance, and civil disobedience. Compassion seeks justice. Justice is compassion politically configured.

In various ways, we can embody compassion. The sentiment of being moved by others' experiences gives rise to concrete acts of restorative care. The heart softened becomes the hand extended. Love takes form.

Signposts for Discerning Compassionate Action

Frequently, the appropriate form through which to embody our compassion is instinctive and self-evident. A neighbor's bout with the flu moves us, and we shuttle her kids to school. We feel joy at a friend's midlife diploma, and we throw a party of pride and celebration. We see a boy with cancer about to become Batkid, and we hop in the car and drive to City Hall to participate. The needs are obvious; our capacities are clear. Compassion becomes kindness without missing a beat.

Other times, discerning compassionate action can be more challenging. We know the need of our neighbor, but we are exhausted keeping up with the needs of our own families. We feel the need to forgive an abuser, but his or her impassive nonrepentance still infuriates us. A person in authority acts unjustly, and compassion feels like giving in. What does compassion look like when fatigue makes the simplest gesture feel overwhelming? Or when a person who has wounded us shows no remorse and we feel not forgiveness but fury? Or when a person has power and wields it oppressively with no signs of letting up?

Actions that embody genuine compassion can sometimes require careful reflection and painstaking discernment. The Compassion Practice offers helpful coordinates in navigating these waters. Compassionate action flows out of the process through which compassion is cultivated. Actions that are genuinely compassionate will resonate with and sustain the healing and renewal that has been nurtured all along the way. Each step of the practice—getting grounded, cultivating Self-compassion, and cultivating compassion for others—offers a signpost to guide our discernment.

The first signpost in discerning genuine compassion is *compassionate action is well-grounded*. Oftentimes actions that appear compassionate, that even mimic the gestures of kindness and goodwill, flow instead from interior movements ungrounded in our compassionate cores. For example, sometimes we care for other people's needs out of the compulsive needs of our own—to be liked, to be necessary, to stay the chilling terror of being alone and undesirable. Or we tirelessly work for compassionate causes—networking with organizations, lobbying institutional leaders, raising public awareness, mobilizing volunteers, serving on the front lines with those who suffer—only to find over time that the springs of compassion that inspired us in the first place have all but withered away. Or burdened with the overwhelming demands of tending a chronically ill family member, we are so fatigued that it takes all we have to go through the motions of giving care while suppressing the resentment that boils deep within us.

Actions that seemingly embody compassion may beat with depleted, distressed, or embittered hearts. While the intentions are admirable, the actions ring hollow. They also ignore the cries of our souls.

Genuine compassion is free and generous, abundant and restorative. It bears a spirit of care and connection that speaks for itself. It flows from the wellsprings of grace and goodwill that ground not only us but also the world. When our impulses to care are uprooted from this soil, our souls let us know. They cry out for rest and renewal. These cries come in the form of resentment, fatigue, compulsive caretaking, numbness, busyness, anxiety, or bitterness. These cries dilute our impulses to care, and moreover, they ache for the U-turn that will hear and restore them.

When our souls are distressed in this way, the most compassionate thing we can do may be withdrawing from the needs of others altogether. We might take some time for ourselves, go on retreat, reconnect with those who remind us of our belovedness, or replenish the reservoirs of life and love from which compassion toward others flows freely. Compassionate actions include those that keep us grounded in the sources of renewal that sustain our spirits and restore our connections. As we return to this ground, we become more available to ourselves and others. Our care for others will flow with abundance, rooted in the renewing soil that holds and sustains us all.

The second signpost in discerning genuine compassion is *compassionate action promotes and preserves the flourishing of our own humanity*. All too often, people are counseled to extend compassion in the midst of relationships that are violating or abusive. A colleague is assaultive with demeaning behavior, and the worker is encouraged to take the high road and endure it with patient understanding. A family gathering includes a former abuser, and the adult survivor is beseeched to forgive and forget and take part in the reunion without dampening its festivity. Or God forbid, a spouse is violent, and the victim is advised to love the batterer and honor the sanctity of marriage by enduring the abuse in silence. These are violations of compassion, not ideals to be lauded and emulated.

Compassion intends to ease suffering and promote the flourishing of life. This includes our own suffering and the flourishing of our own lives. The path of compassion restores us to our Self. It revitalizes the pulse of our spirits. It secures that which we need to survive and sustains the conditions that help us thrive. Only then, out of the abundance of our vitality, is compassion toward others cultivated and embodied. Learning to love others first entails learning to love ourselves.

As such, actions do not embody compassion when they diminish our humanity, minimize our needs for healing and wholeness, leave us vulnerable to violation, silence us, eclipse us, or render us powerless. Sometimes the most compassionate actions we can take are those that embolden our personal power over and against the demands of another. This might include saying no, setting boundaries, asserting our voices, honoring our own needs, claiming space, gathering solidarity, confronting abuse, reporting violations, or securing a season of healing. Through these acts, compassion is still embodied; it is embodied toward us.

The miracle of our souls is that they are pitch perfect in revealing to us what we need to feel safe and vital. In the same way that our bodies feel pain or fever when bruised or infected, our souls communicate with us when something threatens their well-being. The indignation we feel at a demeaning coworker, the rage at a former abuser, the fear of a violent partner, the resistance to the very notion of forgiveness or compassion—these are the cries coming from within guiding us to the source of our personal power. When we do not feel compassion toward others, it is for a good reason. Something within us yearns to be heard. Something aches to know the fullness of life. Compassionate action heeds this cry. It returns us to our Self. It nurtures and sustains the flourishing of our own humanity.

The third signpost in discerning genuine compassion is *compassionate action promotes and preserves the flourishing of others.* This may sound axiomatic. By definition, compassion intends to ease others' suffering and promote their healing and vitality. For a child with cancer, it is rather straightforward. We see his suffering; we are moved by his dignity; and, if our pulses are steady and strong, we respond with caring regard.

Complexities arise, however, with persons whose suffering gives rise to more difficult or even destructive behavior. How do we embody compassion—how do we preserve and promote the flourishing of others—when those persons have perpetrated a crime and remain defiant and unrepentant? Or when those persons hold views with dogmatic condescension that are offensive to us? Or when those persons wield power with relish within a system that is oppressive, unjust, and dehumanizing?

The radical call of compassion says that these too are human beings. They have dignity. They suffer. And their behavior, brutal as it may be, serves as a grotesquely distorted cry of fundamental life-needs that feel threatened or denied. Though it entails the spiritual practice of a lifetime, we can cultivate genuine compassion toward such people. By grounding ourselves in the expansive wellsprings of compassion that hold them and us alike, we can restore the pulse of our reactivities toward them—our fears and resistances, our rages and repulsions—tending to the needs hidden in the cries emanating from our own souls and we can connect empathically with the horrors, indignities, terrors, and self-hatreds that give rise to the abusive and hostile behavior we encounter in others. In short, it is possible to retain our own humanity and to recognize the hidden humanity within them.

That being said, their behavior is destructive, and they need to be confronted. Compassion does not give in to violence. It does not nurture an empathic connection toward others only to justify or tolerate their violation or abuse. It does not allow destructive behavior to continue unchecked. Compassion invites destructive people to return to their own humanity. Promoting and preserving the flourishing humanity of a violent or abusive person includes inviting them into the accountability, self-awareness, and basic regard for others that constitute the core preconditions of authentic human being. Compassion treats them with dignity, and it invites them to live in ways that are true to human dignity.

Warriors of compassion from all over the world have borne witness to what this can look like. By pursuing a radical journey requiring courage and commitment, they demonstrate that promoting the flourishing of destructive people involves treating them with an empathic awareness of their wounded humanity while simultaneously holding firm to the conditions and demands of healthy relationships.

In Tallahassee, Florida, the parents of a teen killed by her boyfriend invite the young man into a process of healing and redemption. They gather with a mediator, a judge, the young man's parents, and a table full of their daughter's heirlooms huddled around her picture. The parents, without minimizing their pain, share their unfathomable grief. The young man, without self-justification, shares his heartbroken remorse and fills in the details, answering every question surrounding the daughter's murder. They agree to a plan for rehabilitation that includes time served, anger management training, and a domestic violence recovery program. He pledges to make symbolic amends—to work in a shelter in homage to the young woman's love for animals and to found an organization devoted to public awareness about the prevalence of teen dating violence.

The restorative justice and tough-love compassion of two extraordinary parents restored a young man's humanity. The parents demonstrate that compassionate action can recognize the suffering of an offender without minimizing the pain he has caused. It can affirm the dignity of someone who has perpetrated a violation while holding him responsible for the consequences of his actions. And it can honor our own needs for healing while inviting the violator into an appropriate relationship—in the case of a violation, a relationship that entails remorse, repentance, rehabilitation, and a commitment to make amends even if only symbolically.[5]

In Brookline, Massachusetts, a man took a shotgun to two abortion clinics, killing two and wounding five. A group of women—leaders within various caucuses on both sides of the issue—realized that the violence had to stop. Equally divided between those committed to pro-choice and pro-life positions, each one with a career devoted to her cause, six of them agreed to meet weekly. Knowing their constituents would feel betrayed for them to be in the same room with their adversaries, they met in secret. Their goal was simple: to dialogue. They would not demonize one another, antagonize one another, or try to change one another's positions. They sought understanding and the possibility of relating across their differences in ways that deescalated public rhetoric and reduced further waves of violence. They told their stories. They shared their fears and longings. They revealed the pain underneath their commitments to the positions for which they fought. And along the way, they saw the humanity in those who once had been their diehard opponents.

For six years, the women met in secret. Then, on the anniversary of the Roe v. Wade decision, they went public. With a united front, they hosted a news conference. They bore witness to the possibility that common ground could be found; caring regard could be cultivated, even with people whose positions remain unequivocally divided. Their meetings were facilitated by the Public Conversations Project, an initiative that sponsors similar conversations across any of a number of divisive topics. These conversations teach persons how to hear and feel the concerns and sensitivities within themselves and within people whose views seem abhorrent. These conversations teach compassion—for our own views and for those of others.

To this day, the six continue to meet. Not one has changed her position on the issue of abortion. But they honor one another's dignity. They oppose one another, but they do so with compassion and even friendship. They demonstrate that compassion bridges enormous ideological divides not with admonition or persuasion but with mutual respect and caring regard for the humanity in one another.[6]

In Nashville, Tennessee, civil rights leaders staged nonviolent protests to end segregation. On a Saturday afternoon, college-aged African Americans courteously but assertively filled lunch counters designated for whites only. The restaurant staff refused to serve them. So the activists sat and did their homework. The second week, the restaurants hired thugs to harass the activists. The thugs spat on them, dropped food on them, and hurled racial epithets at them. Throughout, the activists refused to respond in kind. They were taught to fight hate with love instead of more hate.

The third week, the arrests began. But groups of nonviolent protestors replaced each wave of activists hauled away to the jails. Still, the activists maintained their dignity and treated each party—the police, the thugs, the restaurant staff, the rabid crowds of chanting bystanders—with dignity as well. They knew once segregation was inevitably abolished they would have to share a city together.

Weeks of sit-ins turned into an economic boycott of the entire downtown. Revenues plummeted. The demonstrations multiplied. The home of a prominent African-American attorney was bombed. Finally, the mayor consented to a public meeting. He went on record to say it was time to end segregation. It was time to live together in peace. The restaurant owners, however, had one request. Afraid of national shame and its economic fallout, they asked the civil rights leaders to refrain from making a public announcement lauding their landmark victory. The restaurants would open the counters without drawing attention to it—blacks and whites would simply begin to eat side by side. Foregoing the potential public relations bonanza, the civil rights leaders agreed. Sustaining the dignity of their fellow townspeople was deemed more important than relishing their victory in front of them—as was eating together in peace.[7]

These cases exemplify compassion embodied in radical form. Holding perpetrators of violence accountable while inviting their restitution and restoration to society, listening deeply to the pain and terrors hidden within opponents' position while inviting them to hear that which is hidden within our own, boldly confronting those ensnared within systems of injustice while extending to them the dignity and care that invites them to the table of goodwill and community—these are the actions of warriors of compassion. They seek to understand empathically the suffering and humanity of another. Yet, they are far from sentimental; they are firm. Brutality, abuse, oppression, and vitriol must be checked. These warriors, however, confront such violence with an invitation of compassion. They invite people mired in destructive behavior to claim their own humanity. They offer them the respect and understanding empowered with the backbone of relational responsibility that might touch and transform a heart gone hard.

Tragically, some hearts will remain hard. Perpetrators will remain defiant. Ideologues will be inflexible. Systems of oppression won't yield. At such times, compassion can be moved by the traumas and terrors that breed such calcification, but it still acts with grounded force. Compassion sequesters dangerous people, protects the vulnerable from violation, restrains the assaults of the mean-spirited, and speaks truth to oppressive powers. It does so, however, with dignity. It retains our humanity even in the midst of the inhumane. It honors the humanity within others even when such humanity is hidden.

Warriors of compassion are wise and discerning. They deepen their roots in the soil that sustains them. They tend to the pulse of their spirit, securing what is needed for a restored Self to survive and flourish. And they connect empathically with the pulse of others' spirits, even with those who are offensive and destructive. Then they embody compassionate action. Such action sustains their grounding in the sources of renewal, promotes the flourishing of their own lives and well-being, and promotes the flourishing of others even when such flourishing remains but a distant dream.

Discerning Compassionate Action

Rachel was one of the thousands celebrating Batkid during his victory parade. A software engineer, she was on her way to work when she heard reports of his heroics. She was so moved that she called in to her workplace, took a personal day, and joined the throngs at Union Square. As she watched Miles radiate in the chanting crowd's jubilation, she wept. She clapped, her hands held high, cheered herself hoarse, and wept. Miles's fierce battle with cancer, the city coming together in compassion, getting to be a thread within this extravagant fabric of kindness and goodwill—the entire affair pierced her heart.

Rachel was so overcome that after the rally she was unable to return to work. She walked the city in a fever of tearful euphoria and then holed up in a coffee shop in front of her laptop. She could not shake the story. She Googled every Batkid article she could find on the Internet, poring over the details and tearing up all over again. The stories and photos gave rise to a longing to do something more. She studied the Make-A-Wish Foundation website and searched for other organizations caring for terminally ill children. Those organizations so inspired her that her own work felt meaningless in comparison. She fantasized about walking away from her job and working full time with the sick and the dying. She knew this was absurd—she would be throwing away a career she had worked toward for years—but she daydreamed all the same. She could do hospice care, hospital chaplaincy, perhaps a Peace Corps stint overseas.

For hours, Rachel surfed the Internet, bouncing among Batkid news posts, pictures of caregivers working with children, and listings of opportunities to serve young people battling cancer. She was all but ready to submit her resignation when she realized it was well into the evening. She had lost an entire day stoking the rally's euphoria, captive to the fantasy of giving up everything to work with dying children. Brought back to reality, she was unsure what to make of what was happening within her. Clearly, quitting her job would be rash and irresponsible—she liked her work, and she had no training in caring for children. Yet, writing off the day's events and returning to work as usual felt empty and unsatisfying. Something in the faces of those children moved her. What should she do with the waves of compassion swelling up and overtaking her?

The Compassion Practice provides a path for discerning compassionate actions. Compassionate actions are those that are grounded, flow freely from the steady pulse of our core and caring Self, and nurture the pulse of restored humanity within the persons whose suffering moves us. When actions feel ungrounded, out of sync with a sustained sense of Self-presence, or out of sync with that which is truly restorative for others, they need to be reconsidered, adjusted, and perhaps deferred. Each step of the Compassion Practice helps us know when our actions flow freely with the heartbeat of care or when they are in need of realignment with the pulse of compassion. How might the Compassion Practice aid Rachel in discerning those actions that would ring true for her to embody?

First, it would invite her to *catch her breath*. What began in the morning as an impulse of spontaneous compassion ended by tapping into deeper longings within her straining to get her attention. Somewhere along the way, internal movements hijacked her consciousness. Just as with more violent reactivities like rage or fantasies of revenge, the emotions of euphoria and pathos—even the fantasies of bringing love into the world—can erupt with possessive force and knock us off the ground of Self-awareness. Before leaping into any impulsive action—whether it be quitting her job, enrolling in a chaplaincy program, or slamming her laptop shut on the entire quixotic enterprise—Rachel should first seek solid ground. Catching her breath allows the flurry within to settle. As it does, clarity emerges—not about what to do but about the internal dynamics that need to be tended before she can discern what to do.

Second, Rachel would *take her PULSE*. She would take a U-turn and notice the interior movements activated within her—the waves of tears at the sight of terminally ill children, the compelling urge to tend their wounds, the exuberant joy when they fight for life, the overwhelming impulse to quit her job and care for them full time. She would also notice the internal voice of caution at quitting her job, a misgiving at being untrained for such care, and a reminder that at times she really loves the work she's already doing.

Each of these stirrings is a cry that aches to be heard. Each is rooted in some bid for life that needs to be honored and considered. Discerning compassionate action cultivates a grounded Self-awareness that is free of enmeshment within any one movement and listens deeply to the underlying needs of each one. Extending Self-compassion to these underlying needs and concerns steadies the pulse of our spirits, and it helps us see that which would truly satisfy the deeper yearnings within.

As Rachel listens to the underlying concerns in the flagging cries within her, what might she hear? Perhaps a *fear* that her work has lost its meaning, a *longing* to know that her generative energies touch the lives of the vulnerable in our world, an *aching wound* of a child within her who carries despair and yearns for the care that emboldens the fight for life, or the *gift* of a unique capacity she has to connect with suffering children that has never been named or cultivated. In her cautiousness, she might also hear a longing to remember the sense of meaning her current work originally gave her, a desire that her work with children engage the skills for which she is already trained, or a need that her career—whatever it may be—provides enough material stability to feed and clothe and house herself. Listening to these stirrings with empathic understanding relaxes their intensity and grounds us in the steady pulse of Self-compassion that honors and reassures the deep need of every interior cry. Actions that are most deeply satisfying will ring true within this sense of Self-presence. If something about the action being considered feels off and eludes a sense of interior resonance, some internal concern has not been fully heard and honored.

Third, Rachel would *take the PULSE of the other*. Grounded in Self-compassion, she would turn her attention to the children whose suffering moves her and connect with the needs and yearnings within them. For what do they most deeply long? What do they most need for healing and flourishing in their lives? Which of these needs are already well tended? Which of them still cry out to be heard? Actions that are truly compassionate will be attentive to the genuine needs of those being served. Compassionate action may offer shoes to the barefoot, but it makes sure that the shoes really fit.

The needs of the suffering vary. Like the different forms that compassionate action can take, they include the needs for generosity, service, witness, solidarity, empowerment, and justice. The particular children that Rachel ends up meeting may need, above all else, money to sustain their schooling, a few hours of caring presence, public awareness about their plight, engaging activities during long days of chemotherapy, interactive software to calibrate their medications, or advocacy for the health care denied them. Compassionate action attends to the full range of needs—soulful and social, material and political—that nurture healing and the flourishing of life. Staying empathically attentive and connected to the needs and cries of those by whom we are moved helps us discern those actions that are truly life giving for them.

Fourth, Rachel would *decide what to do*. Of the various ways she could act on her compassion, she would discern which one to embody right now. That action that most rings true will resonate with both the pulse of vitality within her and the pulse of vitality aching to flourish in others. Compassionate actions mutually restore. They nurture and sustain our own flourishing—they utilize our gifts, employ our skills, stimulate our creativity, invigorate our spirits, feed our souls, and deepen our sense of meaning while remaining attentive to the various needs of our general well-being. And they nurture and sustain the flourishing of others—kindling hope, easing pain, empowering resolve, extending networks of support, securing the conditions that enhance well-being, and meeting real needs. Compassionate actions lie at the intersection where life's abundance meets life's diminishment. As Frederick Buechner says of vocation, they are the grounded place where our "deep gladness" meets the world's "deep hunger."[8]

As Rachel considers the compassionate actions that connect her vitality with the needs of others, various acts of care may seem appropriate. She might volunteer a few hours a week at a pediatric cancer unit while keeping her day job to support her. She might volunteer with the Make-A-Wish Foundation and turn another child's dream into reality. She might employ her software gifts for children fighting through cancer in ways that have never been thought of before. Over time she may even decide to take a leave from her job and try out that stint in the Peace Corps. Whatever action she takes, however, will be deliberate not impulsive. It will be restorative both for her and for others—gladness meeting need, life begetting life.

Discerning a particular action does not conclude the process. Rachel can return to the practice. She will recede and get grounded in the renewing springs that sustain her. She will take her PULSE, noticing and tending the stirrings within her that this act of compassion has activated. She will take the PULSE of the persons she has cared for, connecting empathically with the effects of her care and the needs and longings that still linger within them. And then she will discern the next act to take—perhaps a deepened engagement with terminally ill children, enrollment in a program for further training, or a break from it all to tend to herself with compassion.

In this way, the Compassion Practice becomes a continuing cycle. Over time, it becomes a rhythm of life. Actions give way to moments of grounding, to taking our PULSE, to taking the PULSE of others, and to discerning the subsequent restorative act. Acts of compassion give way to personifying compassion—hearts simply beating to the pulse of love.

A Coda for Batkid

After appearing on *Good Morning America* and greeting the mayor of New York, Miles Scott returned to Tulelake. He rejoined his kindergarten class and received a hero's reception. He and his parents teamed with the San Francisco 49ers Foundation to create the Batkid Fund. Through the unexpected worldwide attention, they are raising money for the same organizations that sustained Miles through his battle with cancer.[9] Miles is doing just fine, they say. It is time to turn attention to other children coping with serious illness. In this way, Batkid can now help others.

And so it goes with compassion. Compassion begs to be embodied in acts of care and kindness. Actions without compassion are empty and rote. Compassion without action is ephemeral, warm feeling dissipating into a spiritual vapor.

When embodied, however, compassion can repair the world. Just ask Batkid. He knows. Compassion received becomes compassion extended. The pulse of life resuscitated resuscitates the pulse of life in others. That pulse was beating in a hospital bed in rural California. It beat as well on the streets of San Francisco. Now its beat continues in hearts and hospital beds the world over.

The signs were right. Batkid rocks. He rocks to the beat of compassion.

DISCERNING A COMPASSIONATE

ACTION

Deciding What to Do

1. **Catch your breath**. Ground yourself in whatever way is most helpful to you—listen to music, read a sacred text, light a candle, or sit in a settling silence. Take several deep breaths and ease into an interior space that feels safe, grounding, or sacred.

2. **Take your PULSE**. Once you have settled into a grounding interior space, consider some person or persons to whom you feel invited to extend compassion. This can be a loved one, a coworker, a stranger you've encountered during the day, or a person in your community whose suffering moves you.

   Take a moment and turn inward. Notice what interior movements stir within as you consider the person in your awareness. Welcome and hold any that are there. You might experience pity, fear, anxiety, discomfort at his or her distress, or perhaps measures of your own grief and pain. Assure these interior movements that you are aware that they are present for a reason, and if they prove to be tenacious, you will ponder them more fully. Then invite them to relax so you can be genuinely open and attentive to the person in your awareness.

3. **Take the other's PULSE.**

> *Paying attention.* In your imagination, turn your attention toward the person you feel invited to extend compassion. For a few moments, simply pay attention without judgment to what he or she is doing and the particular way that he or she is doing it as if your observation went without notice.

> *Understanding empathically.* While you continue to gaze upon him or her, cultivate a deeper understanding of the soulful cry hidden within his or her emotions or behaviors. Use the FLAG questions to cultivate this understanding:

> › What *fears* does he or she carry?

> › What *longings* pulsate within him or her?

> › What *aching wounds* haunt him or her?

> › What is his or her hidden and thwarted *gift* yearning to flourish?

> *Loving with connection.* Let yourself feel a sense of compassionate connection to this person. Simply love or care for him or her just as you would love a wounded or frightened child who needs care.

> *Sensing the sacredness.* If it feels right, notice if an expansive sense of sacredness is near and invite that presence—as a healing light, a gentle breeze, a divine figure, an image or symbol—to be with this person at the source of his or her suffering, tending to him or her in whatever way feels healing and restoring.

> *Embodying new life.* Let yourself embrace the new life that yearns to be birthed within the person.

4. **Decide what to do.** Brainstorm various compassionate actions you might embody toward this person. Consider each of the following types of actions and try to list one, two, or even several possible actions under each category.

> Acts of generosity

> Acts of service

> Acts of witness

> Acts of solidarity

> Acts of empowerment

> Acts of justice

Of the various actions that have come to you, be aware of those that most attract, energize, intrigue, surprise, or draw you. Consider that action in light of the signposts of the Compassion Practice:

> Does this action seem to flow from and sustain your own sense of personal and sacred groundedness?

> Does this action promote and preserve the flourishing of your own humanity? Does it flow from your own sense of personal power? Does it maintain and enhance your own human dignity? Does it employ your own unique gifts, skills, and resources? Can you engage in this action without other interior movements or parts of you becoming concerned and activated?

> Does this action promote and preserve the flourishing of the other? Does it maintain and enhance his or her human dignity? Does it meet him or her at the source of his or her deepest and most life-giving needs? Does it contribute to his or her sense of personal power? Does it invite any appropriate need for accountability and restoration?

After pondering these considerations, discern which action feels most resonant with these signposts. What action do you feel most invited to embody toward this person? Which action feels most right?

As a final consideration, imagine yourself engaging in this act of compassion. Like watching a movie, see yourself speaking the words or undertaking the compassionate action that you feel called to embody. Notice what reactions are stirred up within you and sense if they feel resonant with the compassion you feel moved to embody. Notice the effect the action may have on the other person, and sense if it feels resonant with the compassion you feel moved to embody.

If it continues to feel right, extend this compassion into the future encounter you intend to have with this person. Then embody the action itself.

DISCERNING A COMPASSIONATE ACTION

Secret Acts of Compassion for Others

This exercise invites you first to increase your awareness of the various persons in your day—the grocery clerk, the elderly woman who lives down the street, the garbage collector, the bus driver, the man drinking coffee by himself at a coffee shop, a coworker, a family member. Keep your heart and eyes open as you go through the day, and notice the persons you typically encounter. Then choose one person to give your attention to. Who are you most drawn to? Who attracts your curiosity?

As you focus your attention on this person, connect briefly with the PULSE of humanity that beats within him or her in that moment:

> Pay attention to what he or she is doing and how;

> Understand his or her fears, longings, aches, and stifled gifts;

> Love him or her with a quiet sense of connection;

> Sense the sacredness that holds him or her with compassion as well;

> Embody the new life that yearns to flourish within him or her.

Behold the person and his or her PULSE for the few moments you have available while allowing compassion to rise within you. Then listen for an act of kindness that you might undertake toward this person. Maybe you leave a note of gratitude for a waitress. Or maybe you anonymously pick up the check for a person getting coffee. Maybe you get up early and shovel the snow off your neighbor's sidewalk. Or leave freshly baked cookies for the postal worker. Allow your imagination to uncover some secret, anonymous act of compassion to engage in.

After you have completed your secret compassionate act, notice what you experienced as you did it. What did you feel afterward? What are you like when you engage in an act of compassion and kindness?

The Hope

THE MIRACLE OF COMPASSION

Mike was a man who hated Christmas. He believed it brought out the worst in people—the whole greedy lot of them. "When I was young," he grumbled, "Christmas was all about giving. Now it's all about getting. Getting all the toys that you want. Getting to all the sales before others. Getting a bigger bonus than the one you got last year. And I am sick of it. From now on, I want nothing for Christmas. No chocolate samplers, no polyester ties, no bottles of cheap cologne. Until people recognize what Christmas is all about, I don't want to get a thing."

Nan, Mike's wife of some forty-eight years, was worried about him. She worried that his retirement years would be devoured by daytime TV and recliner passivity. And she worried that his cantankerousness would harden and choke off the caring man she knew Mike to be. Surely Christmas, of all times of the year, should be a season in which care could win out over crankiness. And then she got an idea.

The idea came to Nan when she and Mike were watching their grandson's wrestling match. A team of underprivileged teens was in the tournament too. The members of the team were easy to pick out—their uniforms were ragged, their T-shirts threadbare, their sweatpants ill fitting, either too big or too small. And they were being crushed by all of the wealthier schools with crisp and color-coordinated wrestling gear.

"Just look at those boys," Mike bemoaned. "It just isn't right. This sport may be all those boys really have. Sure they jump up after losing but being beaten down over and over again—why it'll take the heart right out of you."

That Christmas, Nan did something different. She tucked a single envelope with Mike's name on it between a few ornaments on the tree. On Christmas morning, after all of the other presents were opened, Nan feigned surprise and said, "Why there's still one more present. And, sweetheart, it has your name on it."

Mike griped, "I thought I said I didn't want anything this year."

"Maybe you'll like this," she prodded.

He took the envelope, eyed it suspiciously, and opened it. Inside was a simple index card. Typed on it was a pledge. During the coming year, Nan would devote her considerable seamstress skills to making wrestling uniforms for the inner-city school the two of them had watched earlier. Mike read it and mumbled, "Well, at least it's not a box of peanut brittle."

Early in January, Nan stayed true to her word. She set up a sewing station in the family room and began sketching uniform designs. After a while, Mike wandered over and glanced at the sketches. He shook his head and scowled, "No, no, no, wrestling uniforms don't look anything like that. Besides, the colors are all wrong. And the sizes, how will you know the sizes unless you know the players?"

"Well, I was wondering about that," Nan admitted. "Do you think you could help me?"

Quicker than a takedown, Mike was off. He went to the school to measure the youngsters. He went to the fabric store to pick out material. He joined Nan in the family room down on the floor to separate fronts from backs and pinning numbers into place.

Of course, more trips to the school were needed. The kids, beside themselves at the idea of new uniforms, begged to be part of the project. Soon, they were selling chocolate bars to buy headgear and scheduling twice-a-day workouts to break in the new equipment. The team adopted Mike and Nan as unofficial team mascots. Mike and Nan took their commitment to the boys seriously and chaperoned away games. They organized a field trip to a tournament at the local university. Mike even took a turn as assistant coach for a day. Sure, he couldn't wrestle like he used to, but he still knew a thing or two about half nelsons and three-point stances.

Mike had so much fun that once the year passed and many of the boys graduated, he started poking around the Christmas tree. His grimace had a glint. "I wonder," he toyed, "if there might be something for me this year." And there was.

Mike and Nan began a new family tradition. Every Christmas played out to the same script. After all the other presents were opened and discarded, Nan would discover a single white envelope lodged in the branches of the tree. With mock surprise she would announce, "Why, Mike, there seems to be something for you after all this year."

Mike would jump up, eye the envelope suspiciously, and muse, "I hope it's not a box of peanut brittle." And it never was. The envelope would hold an index card pledging some project for Mike and Nan to do together during the coming year.

One year Mike and Nan worked at a boys' home designing a playground, organizing car washes to fund it, and mobilizing volunteers to begin its construction. Another year, they galvanized a group of neighborhood children to build birdhouses and feeding stations for wildlife at a local marshland. And one year, they took on city hall. With a band of budding activists, they protested a zoning decision and transformed a vacant lot into a community garden.

Year after year, Mike and Nan carried on. Simple acts of kindness took root throughout the city—at community centers and juvenile halls, at charter schools and children's homes. Each act was germinated by the seed of a single envelope resting on the branch of a Christmas tree. Those envelopes brought life—not only to the town but also to Mike. As Nan would later reflect, "Those were the best years of our lives."

One year, just a few days before Christmas, Mike suffered a stroke and died in his sleep. From all over, family, both close and extended, gathered to attend the Christmas Eve funeral and stay with Nan through her holiday grief. With all of the company, Nan managed to keep herself occupied throughout the day on Christmas Eve. After the funeral, there were meals to cook and linens to put out. As evening approached, there were dishes to wash and coffee to serve. As was her way, Nan rebuffed pleas for her to sit down. And even as the others went to bed, Nan busied herself straightening chairs and setting out breakfast dishes until she and her daughter were the only two still up.

"Mom, it's late, and the kids will be up early. Why don't you get some sleep."

"You go ahead," Nan insisted. "There's a couple more things I want to get done."

"Okay, Mom, but promise me you'll be in bed soon."

"Of course." With a knowing hug, the daughter went to bed.

Nan dug out a few more presents from the closets and stuffed the children's stockings. She checked the Christmas ham and set the timer for the coffee pot. She wiped down the kitchen and locked the back door. Then she switched off the lights room by room until the only light came from the glow of the Christmas tree. And for the first time that day, Nan stopped.

Memories adorned the tree as much as the ornaments. There was the metallic blue ball—the only ornament that hung on the barren tree of Nan and Mike's very first Christmas. There was the embroidered pink cradle with *Baby's First Christmas* lettered on the side. There was the pale green Statue of Liberty, its torch lit red, that Mike just had to have on their trip to New York City. For some time, Nan simply sat and stared, fragments of memories passing before her.

And then, as was Nan's custom, she pulled open the drawer of the end table beside her, and slipped out of a sewing magazine something that had been placed there several weeks earlier. A single white envelope addressed with two words: For Mike. She stared at the envelope for a long time. Then she slid it deep into the branches of the tree.

"This is for you, sweetheart," she whispered. "This is for you."

She pulled the plug on the tree lights and climbed the stairs to bed.

The next morning, squeals from downstairs woke Nan. She had slept longer than she wanted. The rest of the family was already huddled around the tree. She could hear one of her grandkids plead, "When will she be up?"

"Don't worry," a mother reassured. "Grandma will be down soon."

With that cue, Nan donned her robe and slippers and went downstairs. A chorus of greetings rose from the faces that filled her living room.

"Merry Christmas, Mom."

"Merry Christmas, Grandma."

The kids were giddy, and signs of Santa's presence were scattered throughout the room. The tree was lit in all of its festive glory.

And then Nan stopped.

Something was off. It was the tree. It was wrapped in white. Not white lights but white paper. The tree was laden with dozens of white envelopes. All the family members—each daughter and son, granddaughter and grandson, niece, nephew, and cousin—had placed their own envelope on the tree, their own pledge to a project of kindness in memory of Grandpa Mike.

Perched on her stairs that Christmas morning, Nan could already see the ripples of care reaching out into the world. She still ached for Mike. But her grief was eased as she saw not only those Christmas envelopes but also the envelopes multiplying through time on Christmas trees in the future.

And Nan knew how pleased Mike would be. He was, after all, a man who loved Christmas.

The Miracle of Compassion

Sometimes restorative care can be radical—warriors of compassion reaching out to racist segregationists, violent extremists, or the teens who killed their own children. Sometimes, it is as simple as an index card of kindness lodged into the branches of a Christmas tree. Either way, acts of compassion shimmer with the miraculous.

In a world saturated with ideological ill-will, explosive hostility, and soul-killing assault—where abuse bleeds into our homes, our schools, and our sacred institutions; where violence and poverty ravage our cities and neighborhoods; where venom and vitriol permeate our public discourse— any act of kindness and care is a wondrous assertion of humanity within the insidious encroachment of the inhumane.

It is a miracle that a group of women—polarized by something as polemical as abortion—would sit together simply to understand one another and ease the escalation of demonizing rhetoric. It is a miracle that a city would conspire to celebrate the superhero inside of a child standing up to cancer. It is a miracle that an aging wife would see the caring man within her embittered husband and partner with him to complete projects of compassion throughout the final years of their life together.

These are not the spectacular miracles of parting the Red Sea or of raising the dead. They are ordinary miracles—coming from the hands of grandparents and wrestling coaches, mothers, and software engineers. Yet, they are miracles all the same.

These acts suspend the cycles of fear, retreat, attack, and retaliation that play out in our lives with instinctive tenacity. They soften the hearts of those who are hardened, restoring them to their humanity. And they pulsate with sacred presence.

Compassion is holy.

Through acts of compassion, humanity unites with the eternal. The mortal and the transcendent mystically interlace. The life force of the universe beats to the pulse of compassion. When we settle into our caring and connected cores, we move in time with the divine. Our hearts beat as one with the heartbeat of eternity.

Each act of care—be it simple or radical—bears a gift to others or ourselves from the infinite expanse of love that holds all. It is the index card of sacred kindness that we slip into the branches of our broken and beaten-up planet. And when we do so, we can trust that it does not sit there idly; it multiplies. In the morning, we will see. Envelopes of compassion will encompass our world.

Notes

Introduction

1. For a helpful exploration of self-compassion, see Kristin Neff, *Self-Compassion: Stop Beating Yourself Up and Leave Insecurity Behind* (New York: William Morrow, 2011).

2. Karen Armstrong, *Twelve Steps to a Compassionate Life* (New York: Alfred A. Knopf, 2010), 4.

3. One source for this legend is Armstrong, *Twelve Steps*, 50–51.

4. A helpful source on Buddhist compassion is John Makransky, *Awakening through Love: Unveiling Your Deepest Goodness* (Boston: Wisdom Publications, 2007).

5. See Christina Feldman, "Nurturing Compassion," in *The Path of Compassion: Writings on Socially Engaged Buddhism*, ed. Fred Eppsteiner (Berkeley, CA: Parallax Press, 1988), 19.

6. This summation synthesizes the parallel verses of Matt. 5:48 and Luke 6:36 with translations from Walter Wink, *Engaging the Powers: Discernment and Resistance in a World of Domincation* (Minneapolis: Augsburg Fortress, 1992), 267–69, 396.

7. Notable exceptions include John Makransky, *Awakening through Love: Unveiling Your Deepest Goodness*; Thupten Jinpa, *Compassion Cultivation Training* (CCT) in association with The Center for Compassion and Altruism Research and Education (CCARE) at Stanford University; Lobsang Tenzin Negi, *Cognitive-Based Compassion Training* (CBCT) in association with Emory University.

Chapter 1

1. Azim Khamisa, *From Murder to Forgiveness: A Father's Journey* (Bloomington, IN: Balboa Press, 2012). For information on the Tariq Khamisa Foundation, see www.tkf.org.

2. Some suggest that the heart's movement in compassion is more than metaphorical. See, for example, Doc Lew Childre, Howard Martin, and Donna Beech, *The HeartMath Solution: The Institute of HeartMath's*

Revolutionary Program for Engaging the Power of the Heart's Intelligence
(San Francisco: HarperOne, 2000). Ilia Delio cites Mary Jo Meadows
definition of compassion as "the quivering of the heart in response to
another's suffering." *Compassion: Living in the Spirit of St. Francis*
(Cincinnati: St. Anthony Messenger Press, 2011), 47.

3. Burghardt adapted this phrase from one by contemplative Carmelite Fr.
William McNamara. See Walter J. Burghardt, "Contemplation: A Long
Loving Look at the Real," *Church* (Winter 1989): 14–18.

4. See, for example, Phyllis Trible, *God and the Rhetoric of Sexuality*
(Philadelphia: Fortress Press, 1978), 31–59; and *Theological Dictionary of
the New Testament,* vol. 7, s.v. "σπλαγχνον."

5. See David J. Wallin, *Attachment in Psychotherapy* (New York: The
Guilford Press, 2007), 106; and Daniel J. Siegel, *The Developing Mind:
How Relationships and the Brain Interact to Shape Who We Are* (New York:
The Guilford Press, 2001).

6. Though the phrase "U-turn" has been used in numerous contexts, I first
heard it from Richard C. Schwartz, *You Are the One You've Been Waiting
For: Bringing Courageous Love to Intimate Relationships* (Oak Park, IL:
Trailheads Publications, 2008).

Chapter 2

1. The primary source for this story and King's words, which he paraphrased,
is William Johnston, *King* (New York: Warner Books, Inc., 1978), 141–
43. See also, Taylor Branch, *Parting the Waters: America in the King Years
1954–1963* (New York: Simon and Schuster, 1989).

2. For an excellent source on the physiological dimensions of breathing and
well-being, see Alane Daugherty, *The Power Within: From Neuroscience to
Transformation* (Dubuque, IA: Kendall Hunt Publishing, 2008), 114–43.

3. Anthony de Mello, *Sadhana, a Way to God: Christian Exercises in Eastern
Form* (Garden City, NY: Image Books, 1984), 28. See also, Thich Nhat
Hanh *Breathe, You Are Alive!: Sutra on the Full Awareness of Breathing*
(Berkeley, CA: Parallax Press, 2008).

4. Makransky, *Awakening through Love*, 22.

5. Makransky, *Awakening through Love;* Dennis Linn, Sheila Fabricant Linn, and Matthew Linn, *Sleeping with Bread: Holding What Gives You Life* (Mahwah, NJ: Paulist Press, 1995).

6. Genesis 2:7; Psalm 104:29.

7. See, for example, "Breathing the Name of God," in Lawrence Kushner, *Eyes Remade for Wonder: A Lawrence Kushner Reader* (Woodstock, VT: Jewish Lights Publishing, 1998), 144.

8. Gabriel Galache, *Praying Body and Soul: Methods and Practices of Anthony de Mello* (New York: Crossroad, 1998), 19.

9. See Kabir's poem "Professional Counseling" in Daniel Ladinsky, trans., *Love Poems from God: Twelve Sacred Voices from the East and West* (New York: Penguin Compass, 2002).

10. Some, informed by the new cosmology, consider it a morphogenic field of unity and care that permeates the universe. See, for example, Judy Cannato, *Field of Compassion: How the New Cosmology Is Transforming Spiritual Life* (Notre Dame, IN: Sorin Books, 2010).

11. Armstrong, *Twelve Steps*, 3–4.

12. See, for example, Melissa Raphael, *The Female Face of God in Auschwitz: A Jewish Feminist Theology of the Holocaust* (London: Routledge, 2003); Luke 15:11-32; Sandy Boucher, *Discovering Kwan Yin, Buddhist Goddess of Compassion: A Path toward Clarity and Peace* (Boston: Beacon Press, 2000).

13. Helpful descriptions of breath prayers can be found in de Mello, *Sadhana*; Hanh, *Breathe, You are Alive!*; and Tilden Edwards, *Living in the Presence: Spiritual Exercises to Open Your Life to the Awareness of God* (New York: HarperCollins, 1995).

Chapter 3

1. Richard C. Schwartz, *Introduction to the Internal Family Systems Model* (Oak Park, IL: Trailheads Publications, 2001); Richard C. Schwartz, *Internal Family Systems Therapy* (New York: The Guilford Press, 1995). For Merton, while our true self is one of love and compassion, this self is grounded in God as the source of our being; see James Finley, *Merton's*

Palace of Nowhere (Notre Dame, IN: Ave Maria Press, 1978).

2. J. Francis Stroud, *Praying Naked: The Spirituality of Anthony de Mello* (New York: Image Books, 2005), 54.

3. Thich Nhat Hanh, *The Miracle of Mindfulness: An Introduction to the Practice of Meditation* (Boston: Beacon Press, 1987).

4. Anthony de Mello, *Awareness: The Perils and Opportunities of Reality* (New York: Image Books, 1990).

5. Schwartz, *Internal Family Systems* and *Introduction to Internal Family Systems*.

6. Marshall B. Rosenberg, *Nonviolent Communication: A Language of Life* (Encinitas, CA: PuddleDancer Press, 2003), 16–66. Though discovered independently, the Compassion Practice recognizes profound kinship with three other models of human experience that nurture an unequivocal acceptance of and trust in our interior movements: Internal Family Systems Therapy developed by Richard Schwartz; Nonviolent Communication developed by Marshall B. Rosenberg; and Focusing/Bio-Spirituality represented by Eugene Gendlin, Ann Weiser Cornell, Edwin M. MacMahon, and Peter A. Campbell.

7. Coleman Barks, trans., *The Essential Rumi* (San Francisco: HarperSanFrancisco, 1995), 109.

8. The Welcoming Presence Meditation has similarities to Buddhist practices of mindfulness described, for example, in Hanh's *The Miracle of Mindfulness*, and Mary Mrozowski's practice popularly known as the "Welcoming Prayer" taught by Thomas Keating and described in Cynthia Bourgeault's *Centering Prayer and Inner Awakening* (Lanham, MA: Cowley Publications, 2004), 135–52. The essential difference is that the Welcoming Presence Meditation does not "let go" of interior movements but allows them to remain in one's interior space as guests.

Chapter 5

1. See, for example, Melissa Raphael, "When God Beheld God: Notes Toward a Jewish Feminine Theology of the Holocaust" in *Feminist Theology: The Journal of the Britain and Ireland School of Feminist Theology* 21 (May 1999): 62–63.

2. Due to the sexist and hierarchical connotations of the word *kingdom*, Ada María Isasi-Díaz coined the term *kin-dom*. Isasi-Díaz, "Solidarity: Love of Neighbor in the 1980s," in *Lift Every Voice: Constructing Christian Theologies from the Underside*, eds. Susan Brooks Thistlethwaite and Mary Potter Engel (San Francisco: HarperSanFrancisco, 1990), 31–40, 303–305.

3. Marcus J. Borg, *Jesus: A New Vision; Spirit, Culture, and the Life of Discipleship* (San Francisco: Harper & Row, 1987), 125–149.

4. See, for example, Arnold Kotler, ed., *Engaged Buddhist Reader* (Berkeley, CA: Parallax Press, 1996); Eppsteiner, *The Path of Compassion*; Sallie B. King, *Socially Engaged Buddhism* (Honolulu: University of Hawaii Press, 2009).

5. Paul Tullis, "Can Forgiveness Play a Role in Criminal Justice?," *New York Times Magazine*, January 4, 2013 http://www.nytimes.com/2013/01/06/magazine/can-forgiveness-play-a-role-in-criminal-justice.html?_r=0). For a helpful primer on restorative justice, see Howard Zehr, *The Little Book of Restorative Justice* (Intercourse, PA: Good Books, 2002).

6. For more information on this initiative, see, http://www.publicconversations.org, and the historical article there entitled "Talking with the Enemy."

7. For an inspiring documentary chronicling this campaign, see "We Were Warriors," *A Force More Powerful*, directed by Steve York et al. (Princeton, NJ: Films for the Humanities and Sciences, 2000), DVD.

8. Frederick Buechner, *Wishful Thinking: A Theological ABC* (New York: Harper & Row, 1973), 95.

9. For contact information on the Batkid Fund, see https://sf49ers.ejoinme.org/?tabid=504688

Recommended by
The Academy
for spiritual Formation®
THE UPPER ROOM

For those who hunger for deep spiritual experience . . .

The Academy for Spiritual Formation® is an experience of disciplined Christian community emphasizing holistic spirituality—nurturing body, mind, and spirit. The program, a ministry of The Upper Room®, is ecumenical in nature and meant for all those who hunger for a deeper relationship with God, including both lay and clergy. Each Academy fosters spiritual rhythms—of study and prayer, silence and liturgy, solitude and relationship, rest and exercise. With offerings of both Two-Year and Five-Day models, Academy participants redis-cover Christianity's rich spiritual heritage through worship, learning, and fellowship. The Academy's commitment to an authentic spiritu-ality promotes balance, inner and outer peace, holy living and justice living—God's shalom.

Faculty trained in the wide breadth of Christian spirituality and practice provide content and guidance at each session of The Acad-emy. Academy faculty presenters come from seminaries, monaster-ies, spiritual direction ministries, and pastoral ministries or other settings and are from a variety of traditions. Frank Rogers is on the list of faculty for The Academy and currently serves on The Academy Advisory Board.

The ACADEMY RECOMMENDS program seeks to highlight content that aligns with the Academy's mission to provide resources and set-tings where pilgrims encounter the teachings, sustaining practices, and rhythms that foster attentiveness to God's Spirit and therefore help spiritual leaders embody Christ's presence in the world.

Learn more here: http://academy.upperroom.org/.

CPSIA information can be obtained
at www.ICGtesting.com
Printed in the USA
JSHW050333080920
7667JS00003B/6